STUDIES OF INDIAN
JEWISH IDENTITY

STUDIES OF INDIAN JEWISH IDENTITY

Edited by
Nathan Katz

MANOHAR
1995

ISBN 81-7304-071-0

First Published 1995

© Nathan Katz

Published by
Ajay Kumar Jain
Manohar Publishers & Distributors
2/6, Ansari Road, Daryaganj
New Delhi - 110002

Lasertypeset by
A J Software Publishing Co. Pvt. Ltd.
305, Durga Chambers,
1333, D.B. Gupta Road,
Karol Bagh, New Delhi - 110005

Printed at
Rajkamal Electric Press
G.T. Karnal Road
Delhi

Contents

Contents

Introduction

Nathan Katz

When we ask who the Jews of India are, we ask who we are ourselves. When we ask whether they are Jewish or Indian, we ask whether we ourselves are Jewish or American. When we delve into the cultural mechanisms by which India's diverse Jewish communities came to define themselves and how they were defined by others, we explore the very conditions by which a group's identity is established and maintained, how it responds to changing conditions and how it anticipates and structures a future.

All of this is to say that this book is about at least two subjects. First it is descriptive and ethnographic. It describes the beliefs and attitudes, the rituals and histories, which conditioned the identities of three distinct communities of Indian Jews. Second, it is analytical and therefore reflexive; it adheres to the standard of scholarship which insists that in studying the 'other' we learn about ourselves. From the seven essays in this book, what we learn about is identity.

If on the first level we learn about Indian Jewish identity, on another level of abstraction we modify our understanding of Jewish identity worldwide. Our assumptions about Jewish identity as defensive in character, being based on European and American (and occasionally North African or Middle Eastern) Jewish experience, are challenged by Jewish experience in a very different culture.

The Jewish communities studied in this book are diverse, but they have one thing in common: they lived in the palpable absence of anti-Semitism, a cancer unknown in India. These new data compel us to modify our understanding of what it means to be Jewish. It is well-nigh impossible for a Jew of European origin—a Jew with a *shtetl* mentality or with a post-*shtetl* defiance—to imagine a Jewish identity which emerged in an environment which for the most part was hospitable, affectionate and nurturing. Yet, the Jewish experience in India begs us to make this imaginative leap when we henceforth ponder what it means to be Jewish. This book, then, is about Jewish identity in India and how Indian Jewish experience modifies how we understand Jewish identity in general.

But on a higher level of abstraction this book is about how human identity is created, maintained, celebrated and modified. This book's assumption is that the way in which the microscopic communities of Jews in India manage their identity informs our understanding of the issue of identity in the broadest sense.

Historical Background

The essays in this book are about three of India's Jewish communities.[1] The first section is about the Jews of Cochin, before 1947 a princely state and now a port near the southern tip of India on the Arabian Sea. Jews may have come to Cochin as long as two thousand years ago or more, either as traders or as refugees from the Roman sack of Jerusalem. In Cochin they flourished as merchants, agriculturists, soldiers, and in politics—one seventeenth century Jewish leader was simultaneously prime minister to a Hindu maharaja and trading agent for the Dutch East India Company. The Cochin Jews were mostly prosperous, knowledgeable Judaically, and well-positioned in Hindu society.[2]

This section contains two studies. The first chapter by Nathan Katz and Ellen S. Goldberg analyzes Cochin rituals as enactments of identity. Their Indian Jewish identity was shaped by a culture with two traditional sources of status: the royal and the ascetic, reflecting the dominant position of the nobility and of the hereditary priests, respectively. Cochin Jewish observance of the autumn holy days, Simchat Torah in particular, as well as weddings, emphasized the symbolism of royalty. The spring festival of Passover highlighted its ascetic tendencies. Thus, the Cochin Jews' high-caste status was recognizable in their cultural context.

---

[1] For a brief survey of India's six Jewish communities, see Katz and Goldberg, 1988. For an extensive bibliographic study, see Katz, 1991.

[2] On the Cochin Jews, see Katz and Goldberg, 1993 and Johnson, 1985.

Barbara C. Johnson's study analyzes the role played by community parties, or *pestha*, in maintaining group identity by Paradesi Cochini Jews in Israel. What might seem to an untrained observer to be casual and random community parties, when viewed by a trained anthropologist are found to be meaningful and systematic. Johnson skilfully analyzes the profound identity change from being a Jew in India to being a Paradesi Cochini in Israel.

The second section is about the Bene Israel of Maharashtra State, in and around Bombay. But the Bene Israel were in India long before Bombay existed. No one knows when they arrived in India, and they tell of a shipwreck off the Konkan Coast. They lost their books and forgot their Hebrew, became a caste of oil-pressers, lost all contact with other Jews and assimilated into Hindu culture. Nevertheless, they maintained vestigial Jewish observances such that they were eventually "discovered" and made their way back into the Jewish mainstream. Most of them moved to Bombay where they became workers, clerks, civil servants and soldiers.[3]

The second section, too, is comprised of two chapters. The first, by Shirley B. Isenberg, succeeds at the very difficult task of entering into the world of the Bene Israel of the villages of the Konkan. This undertaking is especially difficult because, for the most part, the Bene Israel have become quite modernized, and the village life Isenberg explores is pre-modern. Skilfully analyzing interviews with elderly Bene Israel, as well as government and mission records, she manages to provide a portrait of the inner world of the Bene Israel prior to migration to Bombay.

Joan G. Roland's piece complements Isenberg's because it analyzes the profound changes in Bene Israel identity over the past two centuries. Once an obscure oil-pressing caste scattered throughout the Konkan's villages, they are now modern, urban Jews. The influences which precipitated such huge changes were encounters with Jews from Cochin, Christian missionaries, British bureaucracy, Baghdadis in Bombay, and the worldwide Zionist move-

[3]The best scholarly studies of the Bene Israel are Isenberg, 1988 and Roland, 1989.

ment. Roland's essay describes how these external influences modified the internal sense of identity of the Bene Israel.

Our third section is about the Baghdadis—Arabic-speaking immigrants to British India who lived in India but were never of India, unlike the Cochin Jews who were well acculturated and the Bene Israel who had become assimilated. The Baghdadis were industrialists, traders and financiers who settled in British India's leading port cities: Bombay, Calcutta and Rangoon (now in Burma). The Baghdadis remained aloof from Indianness; English replaced Arabic as their mother tongue with no intermediary of Hindusthani, which they used only for trade and to speak with servants.[4] Thomas Timberg's chapter explores how and why the Baghdadis remained aloof from things Indian as they identified with their British overlords in an ill-fated attempt at assimilation into a world which, ultimately, would not accept them.

Ruth Fredman Cernea's study concentrates on Jewish life in Rangoon. Like their brethren in Bombay and Calcutta, Rangoon's Jews were mostly Baghdadis but counted a few Cochinis and Bene Israel among their number. As in Bombay and Calcutta, Rangoon was the scene of bitter disputes which emerged between the dominant Baghdadis and their coreligionists who were distinct ethnically. Cernea's essay is enriched by memories, interviews and diaries which portray a charming, if flawed, Judaic life in Burma which is no more.

The fourth section describes the situation of all three communities—the Cochin Jews, the Bene Israel and the Baghdadis—as Indian Jews become increasingly marginal. Religious observances and community identity suffer from the lack of a critical mass which sustains Jewish communal life. While the Bene Israel of Bombay still number more than five thousand, sufficient for communal life, assimilation into modern, urban culture threatens to engulf them.

Margaret Abraham describes the disintegration of identity experienced by many Indian Jews, mirroring the disintegration of

---

[4]On India's Baghdadi Jews, see Timberg's two articles in Timberg, ed., 1986; see also Ezra, 1986 and Musleah, 1975.

their beloved communities. As family member after family member immigrates to Israel (or to Britain, Australia, Canada or the U.S.), communal life as well as religious observances become attenuated. With the notable exception of Bombay (and perhaps in Manipur and Mizoram, who can say?), Jewish life in India is nearly extinct. Abraham's chapter is a dispassionate analysis of a painful reality.

There were and are other Jewish communities in India which are not the subject of chapters in this book. One community about which we know very little were the so-called Mughal Jews, Persian-speaking courtiers of the Mughals and itinerant traders and mystics who originated mostly in Afghanistan and Persia.[5]

Another are the Ashkenazim. For centuries, a trickle of Eastern European fortune-seekers, refugees and mystics found their way to India, attaching themselves to existing Jewish communities. Significant numbers of Ashkenazim who were fleeing Hitler made their way to India, where thousands waited out Europe's madness, and a few remain today. The story of India in the Holocaust remains to be told, and must be done soon before those who remember are gone.[6]

Finally, there are enigmatic communities of tribal people in far northeastern India, in Manipur and Mizoram, who claim to be a lost tribe of Jews. More than that, many have undergone orthodox conversion to Judaism. They have built synagogues, learned Hebrew, perform life-cycle rituals, and live Jewish lives as best they can.[7]

Ethnicity, Nationality, Community or Peoplehood?

In America, a group's identity is understood as "ethnicity". In Europe, "nationality" is virtually synonymous with the American ethnicity. To avoid confusion, scholars distinguish between nation-

---

[5]Information about the Mughal Jews is sketchy, at best. The standard work on the subject is Fischel, 1949.

[6]The story of the Ashkenazim has not yet been written.

[7]On the mysterious tribals, see Samra, 1991.

ality and citizenship, the latter a legal and political concept and the former an organic, cultural term. In India, the same idea is conveyed through "community". The Jewish parallel is "peoplehood".

All of these concepts—ethnicity, nationality, community cr peoplehood—are fluid, which is to say they are products of culture, adapt to social, economic and political change, and embody distinctions deemed significant by a culture. In days gone by, the categories were hard and rigid, unchanging and genetically determined: "race" in the Western world, and "caste" (*jati*) in India.

The difference between the modern understanding of group identity and the traditional way is that today's approach emphasizes the plasticity of identity and the huge role culture plays in shaping our sense of ourselves. According to more traditional views, whether Indian or European, identity is a fact but not an act, it is transmitted at or before birth and is with us, indelibly and unalterably, throughout our lives and is passed on to our children.

Strategies for Analyzing Indian Jewish Identity

In these studies of Indian Jewish identities, we encounter both approaches. The former, modern understanding pervades our essays. It is the presupposition, stated or otherwise, of all modern scholarship.

Yet, it should surprise no one that in describing themselves (or in being described by their Hindu, Muslim or Christian neighbors), traditional categories abound. Thus, some of India's Jews were a caste within India's regional hierarchies. In fact, the Indian term for caste, *jati*, is a cognate of the Latin genus, a biological rather than a cultural concept. All of India's Jews either emphasized their *yichus*—blood descent from ancient Israel—or attacked other Jews for their lack of *yichus*. The biological categories of Jewish and Hindu culture overlapped at times, establishing a comfortable biological identity among groups who likewise assumed their own identity was biological.

Modern scholars hold that ethnic identity (to use the American terms, which may bear subtle differences from analogous European, Jewish or Indian concepts) is dynamic and interactive. That is, it changes as historical circumstances change, and it changes depending on its audience and its aims.

The Trajectory into History

Indian Jewish identities, of course, are conditioned by the past. When asked to say who they are, a group, like an individual, is likely to tell a story. Their legend may or may not be factual; most likely, it interweaves facts with speculations, and it grafts itself onto other, perhaps better-known legends. For example, both the Cochin and Bene Israel Jewish communities of India graft the story of their life in India onto the sacred time of the Biblical, normative Jewish story. Thus, they were traders from King Solomon's court; or, they were a lost tribe from the Assyrian conquest of Israel in the eighth century B.C.E.; or, they fled the Roman occupation of Jerusalem and the destruction of the Temple in 70 C.E.; or they fled persecutions in fifth century Persia; or they were merchants from Yemen.

In his study of the state theater in Bali, Clifford Geertz pondered the seeming unreliability of indigenous history and wrote: "Not only are the data scattered, equivocal, and all too often poorly presented; but the mode of interpreting them . . . . has been . . . . sociologically unrealistic in the extreme . . . . [These accounts] have led to a picture . . . . which, though not without its elements of plausibility, perhaps even truth, has about it the unmistakable air of fantasy systematized which derives from attempting to know what one has no way of knowing" (Geertz, 1980:25).

But that is just the point. Historical legends, like myths and personal narratives (autobiographies, psychiatric patients' stories, conversion testimonies, confessions, etc.), derive their cognitive power precisely from their being attempts at knowing "what one has no way of knowing". The power of these legends lies not in their conformity with facts but, on the contrary, historical narratives derive their power precisely because their factuality is secondary to their cognitive power, the ability to shape and provide a framework for the vicissitudes of life.

Social Trajectories: Reaching Outward

Identity is not only a matter of the past, it is a reality of the present.[8] Of course, memories and legends are not properly in the domain of the past. They are present-day assemblages created out of fragments of a past which could not be known in full; which is to say our legends are at least a little bit nostalgic.

But there is more to identity than narration. Identity is created by a group's interactions with other groups, just as an individual's identity is in part a product of his or her social network. Who one is, is a function of with whom one associates and the quality of those associations. Fredrik Barth noted that ethnic identity organizes interactions with members of other groups (1969:10). The data about Indian Jews suggest a more dynamic, interactive model: ethnic identity conditions and is conditioned by social interactions.

Thus, our seven chapters analyze how India's Jews interacted with their neighbors, with the society in which they found themselves. Highly significant were the Jews' relationships to political power: with local maharajas in Cochin, with Muslim nawabs of the Konkan, or with British colonial powers in Bombay and Calcutta. Contact with local religious elites, such as the Nambudiri Brahmins of Kerala, as well as contact with the religious life of ordinary people, which were especially significant for the Bene Israel, are described. In both cases, the religious life as well as the social position of the Jews were modified.

Of equal significance was how one Jewish community inter-

---

[8]George De Vos, too, observed that identity is created out of orientations based on the present, future and past. While we emphasize the interactions among these time-orientations in the construction of Indian-Jewish identities, De Vos understood this time-orientation as a choice between political, religious or ethnic identities. He wrote (1970:8-9): "[E]thnicity .... relates .... not only to one's place in the status system, but also to internal conflicts over the priority to be given to past-, present-, or future-oriented forms of self-identity .... [A]n individual can lean toward one of three orientations: (1) a present-oriented concept of membership as citizens in a particular state . . . ; (2) a future-oriented membership in a transcendent, universal religious or political sense; or (3) a past-oriented concept of the self as defined by one's ethnic identity, that is, based on ancestry and origin."

acted with other Jewish communities. For example, the Baghdadi Jews of Bombay aspired to the "European" status of the British. Since the British condescended towards anything "Indian", the Baghdadis came to condescend towards their Bene Israel coreligionists, who were highly Indianized. Similarly, the Sephardim who came to Cochin during the sixteenth century discriminated against local Jews who had preceded them by perhaps 1,500 years. Whether in Rangoon, Cochin, Bombay or Calcutta, the courts of the land heard complaints of discrimination made by Jews against other Jews.

Goal-oriented Trajectories: The Future

The future also conditions the present. For example, how the Bene Israel defined their relationship with worldwide Jewry, Zionism in particular, was an instance of a group's aspirations for the future modifying their understanding of the present. The story of the Bene Israel is fascinating in part because of the dramatic shifts in their self-understanding;—shifts occasioned by contact with other Jewish groups. First was their "discovery" by the Cochin Jew, David Rahabi, in the eighteenth century. Second were their ambivalent relationships with the Baghdadis. And finally, they were most profoundly influenced by Zionism, an influence which led most of them to immigrate to Israel.

So, too, Indian nationalism, a polar force in the experience of Indian Jews, and complementary to Jewish nationalism, or Zionism, shaped the identities of India's Jews from Cochin to Calcutta. Asian Jews, especially in Iran and other Muslim nations, had come to view the British in quasi-messianic terms: the British were their beloved liberal liberators. At the same time, Jews enjoyed amicable, respectful relationships with their Indian neighbors of all religions. The question before them was: with whom to identify in the struggle between their two friends, the British and the Indians? Paradoxically, they loved Gandhi at the same time as they admired Churchill—who, after all, was the Jews' champion against Hitler.

In India, the Jews are perceived, and perceive themselves, as

Jews. In Israel, they are perceived as Indians—or to be more precise, as Bene Israel, as Paradesis, and as Cochinis. In a new context, new strategies for identity are being devised and enacted.

Ritual Enactments of Identity

In has long been recognized that religion often plays an important, even determining, role in identity (De Vos, 1970:13-15). For example, long-suppressed religiously conditioned identities are reshaping eastern Europe and much of central Asia today. But our question precisely is : how does religion function to establish, define and maintain identity. To address this question, we must consider specifically the role of ritual as an enactment of identity.

Thus, this book analyzes Indian Jewish identity as a complex product of four interrelated phenomena. First, there is the historical trajectory, the construction of a suitable narrative. Second, there are the social trajectories of the present, the patterns underlying social interactions with Gentile neighbors, which also defined the group. Third, there are the trajectories of the future, which is to say how modernization, Zionism and Indian nationalism came to reconstellate Jewish identity by directing it toward new, sometimes competing, goals. Finally, there is the role of religion, not merely as a template of ethnic identity but as a system of rituals and norms which defined and celebrated the very identities of India's Jews.

The Book

With the exception of Isenberg's and Johnson's chapters, all of the essays in this book were first presented in a panel on "Indian Jewish Identity" at the annual meeting of the American Academy of Religion in New Orleans in 1990, which was organized by this writer. There are not very many scholars who concentrate on Indian Jewry, and this was the first time so many had convened for discussion. The panel was comprised of scholars trained in the fields of sociology, anthropology, history, economics and religious studies; yet commonality in issues and interests—as well as subject matter—was more significant than diversity of discipline. In fact, the panelists felt that such a multidimensional and complex phenomenon as ethnic identity would benefit from a continuing discussion from such diverse disciplinary perspectives.

The panel participants, besides myself, were Roland, Timberg, Cernea and Abraham. The papers were revised, benefitting from each other's current work, and Johnson and Isenberg were invited to join in this book. Not only did all panelists admire Johnson's and Isenberg's contributions to the field, but the foci of their research complemented the papers by the panelists, providing as comprehensive a study of Indian Jewish identity as possible in one volume.

Sources cited

Barth, Fredrik, ed. 1969. *Ethnic Groups and Boundaries: The Social Organization of Culture Difference.* Bergen-Olso: Universitets Forlaget and London: George Allen & Unwin.

De Vos, George. 1970. "Ethnic Pluralism: Conflict and Accommodation," pp. 3-41 in George De Vos and Lola Romanucci-Ross, eds. *Ethnic Identity: Cultural Continuities and Change.* Palo Alto, CA: Mayfield.

Ezra, Esmond David. 1986. *Turning Back the Pages: A Chronicle of Calcutta Jewry.* London: Brookside Press.

Fischel, Walter J. 1949. "Jews and Judaism at the Court of the Moghul Emperors in Medieval India," *Proceedings of the American Academy for Jewish Research* 18:137-177.

Geertz, Clifford. 1980. *Negara: The Theatre State in Nineteenth-Century Bali.* Princeton University Press.

Isenberg, Shirley B. 1988. *India's Bene Israel: A Comprehensive Inquiry and Sourcebook.* Bombay: Popular Prakashan.

Johnson, Barbara C. 1985. " 'Our Community' in Two Worlds: The Cochin Paradesi Jews in India and Israel." Unpublished Ph.D. dissertation, University of Massachusetts.

Katz, Nathan. 1991. "An Annotated Bibliography about Indian Jewry," Kol Bina 8, 1:6-33.

Katz, Nathan, and Ellen S. Goldberg. 1988. "The Last Jews in India and Burma." *Jerusalem Letter* 101:1-8.

Katz, Nathan, and Ellen S. Goldberg. 1993. *The Last Jews of Cochin: Jewish Identity in Hindu India.* Columbia, SC: University of South Carolina Press.

Musleah, Ezekiel N. 1975. *On the Banks of Ganga: The Sojourn of Jews in Calcutta.* North Quincy, MA: Christopher Publishing.

Roland, Joan G. 1989. *Jews in British India: Identity in a Colonial Era.* Hanover, NH: University Press of New England.

Samra, Myer. 1991. "The Tribe of Manasseh: 'Judaism' in the Hills of Manipur and Mizoram," *Man in India* 71:183-202.

Timberg, Thomas A., ed. 1986. *Jews in India.* New Delhi: Vikas.

Part I

The Cochin Jews

1

The Ritual Enactments of
Indian-Jewish Identity of the Cochin Jews[1]

Nathan Katz and Ellen S. Goldberg

In any discussion of the Cochin Jews,[2] the question inevitably arises: Are they Jewish or are they Indian? This essay will demonstrate that this question is inappropriate. It embodies cultural presuppositions entirely alien to the lived world of the Cochin Jews. Just as no American Jew would be at pains to neatly demarcate—or even recognize—where Jewishness begins and Americanness ends, so the Cochin Jew is hurt when there is an attempt to bifurcate his or her cherished identity. The unique *minhagim* (local customs

[1]Field research for this study, conducted during the Hebrew year 5747 (1986-87), was made possible by a Fulbright senior research grant, a University of South Florida President's Council grant, and several University of South Florida Research and Creative Scholarship awards. This article is a revised version of "The Ritual Enactments of the Cochin Jews: The Powers of Purity and Nobility," which appeared in *Jouranl of Ritual Studies* 4, 2 (1990): 199-238, which incorproated material from "Asceticism and Caste in the Passover Observances of the Cochin Jews," *Journal of the American Academy of Religion 57*, 1 (1989):53-82, and an extended analysis of the observances of the Cochin Jews is found in Nathan Katz and Ellen S. Goldberg, *The Last Jews of Cochin: Jewish Identity in Hindu India* (Columbia: University of South Carolina Press, 1993).

[2]The Cochin Jews are one of six distinct Jewish communities who have made their home in India. The others are: (1) the Bene Israel of Maharashtra state, especially in Bombay city; (2) the Persian-speaking traders and courtiers of the Mughal period; (3) the Arabic speakers, mostly from Iraq and Syria, who settled in Bombay, Calcutta, and Rangoon during the time of the British Raj, known as "Baghdadis"; (4) the Russian-, German-, and Yiddish-speaking Ashkenazim, many of whom came as refugees from Hitler's Europe; and (5) the mysterious Chin-kuki tribals of Manipur, Mizoram, and Assam states of India, Chin state in Burma, and Chittagong hill tracts of Bangladesh, who claim to be the remnant of the tribe of Menashe (Katz and Goldberg, 1988).

or observances of Jewish law) of Cochin, developed over more than a millennium, can be understood as the ritual establishment and celebration of Indian-Jewish identity.

The Westerner invariably misapprehends the Cochin Jew's identity. Because visitors to Jew Town[3] are most often either Western Jews with little appreciation of India, or Indians with little knowledge of Jewishness, no one has yet described Cochini identity as both *fully* Indian and *fully* Jewish. In part this problem is due to the disciplinary fields of study found in Western universities, fields that inelegantly divide up the world into an East and a West. The Cochin Jews have been approached academically from the point of view of Jewish studies and from the point of view of South Asian studies. However, for the Jew Town folks, Indianness and Jewishness are not neatly-bounded fields of study, but rather together they form a seamless universe of meanings, customs, aesthetics, and rituals. The following analysis of their observances will attempt to show that the Cochin Jews are both Jewish and Indian, and fully so.

In India social identity means social position, power, and place. Whereas for Hindu castes, social position is a given, but for extrinsic castes it must be established ritually. The Cochin Jews' observances, especially the idiosyncratic and exotic aspects of their

---

[3]"Jew Town" is an area immediately south of the palace of the Maharaja of Cochin in Mattancheri. It consists of one long, north-south street, now called Synagogue Lane, culminating in a cul-de-sac at the lane's northern end. The synagogue abuts and shares a courtyard wall with the maharaja's private Pazhayannur Sri Krsna temple. Cochin is the largest city and major port of the modern state of Kerala, known in medieval geography as Malabar, but the name Cochin is ambiguous. It is used to refer to the independent principality ruled by a succession of maharajas until its amalgamation into the Union of India in 1948. Likewise, it is the name for a small, British (originally Portuguese, then Dutch) settlement two miles north of Mattancheri, where the Cochin Jews live, at the mouth of the Bay of Cochin and which is now known as Fort Cochin. It is also the name of the contemporary municipality encompassing Fort Cochin, Mattancheri, the modern seaport of Ernakulam located across the Bay, a huge naval base, the home of the Southern Command of the Indian Navy, and several islands, including Vypeen and the artificial Willingdon island.

minhagim, have served to locate them within Kerala's complex caste system. This has been accomplished by ritually enacting and appropriating Indian symbols of power.

Among the most distinctive features of Indian civilization are two separate sources of power, social prestige and position. Ever since Manu's fourth-century codification of social law, the Brahman priests and the nobility—usually Ksatriyas, but in Kerala the Nayars—have derived status from these two sources: the ascetic and the princely. The Brahmans, who occupy one of the two apexes of the Indian hierarchy, are distinguished by symbols of purity: their pure food, white clothes, ascetic life-style, and their self-distancing from such sources of pollution as animal carcasses and meat, lowly-born people, and agriculture. This distance has been maintained through an intricate, hierarchical system of social interdependence, customs, and taboos. Such purity is deemed an essential prerequisite for the efficacious re-enactments of ancient rituals that constitute the Brahmans' means of livelihood. In Kerala the chaste rituals of the Nambudiri Brahmans, the religious elite, are counterbalanced by the colorful, riotous deity processions of the Nayars, who are the dominant caste, politically and economically. The Nayars' object of worship is not some abstract metaphysical concept, but rather the life-embracing, erotic warrior-prince god, Lord Krsna, who embodies the Ksatriya ideal.

The nobility, the second apex of the Indian hierarchy, have traditionally employed the symbols of royalty, conquest and wealth. Not the homespun white cotton of the Brahman, but fine silks and jewels bedeck the Ksatriyas and the maharajas.

In their *minhagim*, the Cochin Jews have placed in the foreground the symbols of purity and nobility inherent in Judaism at the same time as they have adapted some of the priestly and royal symbols of Hinduism, making for one of the most exotic systems of Jewish observance found anywhere in the Diaspora. On the one hand, they have appropriated certain Brahmanical symbols of purity in their unique Passover observances. On the other hand, they have adapted aspects of the Nayars' symbols of royalty and prosperity in their unique Simchat Torah[4] observances as well as in their marriage customs.[5] Moreover, they managed this syncretism judiciously so as not to contravene *halacha*.

Halacha, Jewish law, is the systematization of ethical, social, and ritual norms that have defined Jewish practice since the establishment of the rabbinic academy at Yavneh following the destruction of the Second Temple in 70 C.E. *Minhag* is the way *halacha* is observed according to local customs, and *minhagim* vary from place to place. *Halacha* is incomplete without *minhag*. Jewish law is not sufficiently specific and detailed so as to serve as an exhaustive guide for many Jewish observances, especially the life-cycle rituals. *Halacha* provides the framework, but one would be unable to celebrate a *brit milah, a bar mitzvah*, a wedding, or a funeral unless one relied upon local *minhagim* (Chill, 1979:vii). To put the point in the traditional idiom, *halacha* as Oral Torah is God's imperative, and *minhagim* are creative human responses to that imperative.

Judaism's adaptations to various cultures have gone beyond these *minhagim*. Like all truly ancient religions, Judaism is extremely complex, comprising diverse threads over centuries and millennia. Unique among the world's religions is Judaism's diasporization; Jews have lived as guests—welcome or otherwise—among all people of the world. Since Jewish tradition is so multidimensional, depending upon the Jews' host culture, differing aspects of Jewishness have come to the fore, and other aspects relegated to the background. In Protestant America, for example, Judaism's prophetic threads have been brought to the foreground, and according to some Jews in America Judaism is reducible to

---

[4]Hebrew has been Romanized according to the system proposed in Weinberg in 1976, except when the sweet-sounding Cochin pronunciation is rendered phonetically, as in *massa* instead of *matsah, hamas* instead of *chamets*, and so on.

[5]Cochin marriage observances, like Simchat Torah observances, evidence Nayar borrowings; however, in this essay only calendric festivals are analyzed. The reader is directed to *The Last Jews of Cochin: Jewish Identity in Hindu India*, for a discussion of rituals and identity which includes such life-cycle events as *brit milah* (circumcision), *bar mitzvah*, and weddings.

ethics. In Hindu India, however, it is the Jewish priestly-ascetic and noble-kingly threads that have been emphasized, and the fiery ethical imperatives of the prophets have been less central. Certainly no Indian Jew would understand the prophetic threads as in themselves constitutive of Jewishness—but an American Jew might.

Judaism has ample indigenous resources that could easily be assimilated to Brahmanical priestly-ascetic symbols, including: (1) a hereditary priesthood of *kohanim*, paralleling the Brahmans; (2) a fastidious system of the laws of *kashruth*, or dietary regulations; (3) complex laws governing family purity; and (4) ascetic tendencies in certain holidays, especially Passover and Yom Kippur. At the same time, Judaism has other resources comparable to the noble-kingly symbols of the Nayars, including: (1) the royalty symbolism (*malchut*) of the High Holy Days; (2) the resemblances between the Torah processions (*haqafot* or rodeamentos) of Simchat Torah and Hinduism's deity processions; and (3) the royalty symbolism traditionally ascribed to brides and bridegrooms. The *minhagim* of the Cochin Jews represent a creative synthesis that accentuates Jewish traditions connected with these two symbol complexes, while at the same time incorporating comparable elements from Hindu traditions. The following analysis will briefly examine the Cochin Jews' appropriation and adaptation of priestly-ascetic symbols of power as enacted in Passover preparations and observances, and of the noble-kingly symbols of power as ritually displayed at Simchat Torah.

There is more to this study than an ethnographer's cataloging of exotic customs, charming as that undertaking may be. The fascination of studying an Indian Jewish community implies a reconsideration of Judaism in its better known contexts. Fresh and import questions arise. From the perspective of Jew Town in Hindu Cochin, for example, American Judaism looks very Protestant and very Amercian. This is because it is never simply the "other" that is the object of scholarship, but always the understanding of self.

The Cochin Jews and the Caste Hierarchy

The ritual observances of the Cochin Jews serve as a means of periodically reaffirming their status in the Indian caste hierarchy. Before turning to an analysis of these rituals, we must therefore briefly consider their relation to the caste system and in particular to the two groups whose symbols they have appropriated: the Nambudiri Brahmans and the Nayars. First, we must ascertain in what ways the Cochin Jewish community resembles a caste, or emulates caste behavior. In this context certain methodological questions about caste must be considered: what do we mean by caste? Is caste a function of Hindu sacralization, a somewhat idealized view, or does caste reflect the material more than the religious realities of South Asia? Second, we must consider where to place the Jews within Kerala's caste system. Here we need to distinguish between "attributional" and "interactive" approaches to caste ranking: the former views caste in terms of intrinsic attributes, whereas the latter concentrates on the interrelations between and among castes as the key to determining a group's status.

The case of the Cochin Jews is a notable exception to the "rule" of caste behavior postulated by Dumont: "there are two main avenues whereby a foreign group could enter a territorial set of castes. One is at the level of the Untouchable . . . . The other possible avenue into a caste system is at the level of dominance" (1980:193). In fact, the Jews' position in the hierarchy is somewhere between the dominant groups and the untouchables, although they are considerably closer to the dominant Nayars and Nambudiri Brahmans.

The term *jati*, derived from the root *jan* or *ja*, "to be born," conveys the sense of "nature", "character", or "class" in the biological sense (Edgerton, 1977:240). According to accepted scholarly analysis, castes can be distinguished by three characteristics: "*separation* in matters of marriage and contact, whether direct or indirect (food); *division* of labour, each group having, in theory or by tradition, a profession from which its members can depart only within certain limits; and finally *hierarchy*, which ranks the groups as relatively superior or inferior to one another" (Dumont, 1980:21).

In their separation from other groups, the Cochin Jews obviously exhibit caste behavior, which they maintain through endogamy and dietary restrictions. They are in a somewhat ambiguous position with respect to their observance of *kashruth*. On the one hand, the very existence of a strict and complex dietary code bestows high status. On the other hand, the presence of meat in their diet resembles low-caste practices. However, meat is eaten only in the home, which is the only place where *kosher* meat is available. In public the Cochin Jews frequent Brahman vegetarian restaurants, which meet the strictest requirements of *kashruth* while at the same time reinforcing their high social position.

As for hereditary occupations, we simply do not have adequate evidence available to reach definitive conclusions. In modern times the Cochin Jews have been professionals (attorneys, professors, engineers, teachers, physicians), merchants large and small, and clerks. We know that in the past, from the sixteenth century until the vigorous land redistribution policy undertaken by Kerala's Communist government in 1957, most of the community's income was derived from coconut estates owned by the synagogue and by leading Jewish families, the Halleguas in particular. Landholding was the main criterion by which the dominance of a caste such as the Nayars was exercised, according to accepted theory ("Caste", 1987:3-4). The Cochin Jews were also international spice merchants. We have meagre evidence about their life prior to their fleeing from Cranganore in the fourteenth to sixteenth centuries, where they were primarily agriculturists and warriors. In general, however, occupation has not played a major role in the Cochin Jews' identity, at least as they have understood it. "Work, for many of them. . . ," wrote Mandelbaum, "was necessary and even meritorious in its proper time and place, but was a practice that should not stand in the way of ritual devotion or pleasure" (1981:226).

Finally we come to the issue of hierarchy: How has the group been perceived by other groups within the dynamics of Kerala society? We shall consider this issue later in our discussion of Passover.

Dumont (1980:43) views these three components of caste—separation (endogamy and food), division of labor (occupation) and hierarchy (status)—as aspects of one overarching principle of purity as against pollution. As we shall see, the Cochin Jews' concern with purity at Passover is excessive by the normative Jewish standard of *halacha*, and this excess is best understood as a function of the Cochin Jews' concern to maintain their high status in the caste hierarchy.

Any group in India which has its own endogamous marriages, food restrictions, ritual language and calendar, and which is accepted as Indian, ought to be considered a caste. However, there has been some scholarly squeamishness about considering the Cochin Jews a caste because they follow a foreign religion and claim a foreign origin. Some scholars hold that the caste system is a unique manifestation of Hinduism, sacralized in the *Rg Veda* and expounded in the *Dharmasastras*—such as *Manu Smrti*—as the basis for society (Dutt, 1977). This view stresses the uniquely Hindu nature of caste, and non-Hindu groups such as Muslims, Sikhs, Christians, and Jews are seen in this perspective more as variants of the caste system than as castes proper. In any case, their behavior has been viewed as problematic and eccentric. In fact, David Mandelbaum (1939) is the only scholar to refer explicitly to the Cochin Jews as a *jati*. How, it was asked, could an egalitarian religion such as Judaism adopt such nonegalitarian, hierarchical practices? Our data suggest that this is the wrong question to ask.

As the archetypal Brahman, Manu articulated in his writings a specifically Brahman ideology of caste. His concern was the establishment of a sacred social order with his community at the apex. To do so he employed a specifically religious ideology, one rooted in texts we have come to associate with Hinduism. It would be superficial to maintain that all segments of Indian society accepted Manu's vision of a sacred social order or to hold that caste was rooted only in ancient texts. Such a textual view of a civilization can be highly misleading.

Further complications arise from foreign perceptions of India. As strange as it may seem, the very term "Hindu" is what misleads us. It is a highly reified and very non-Indian concept. The term is geographic in origin and not religious. It was first coined by the eleventh-century Muslim Ghaznavad invader Mahmud to refer to the inhabitants of the land beyond the Indus River, which he crossed en route from Afghanistan to the Punjab. In short, "Hindu" was the Muslim invaders' perception of India, not an Indian self-perception. Similarly, the concept of "Hinduism" is a British construct. Just as "Hindu" was originally a Muslim concept, the notion of "Hinduism" was the British attempt to impose order, first conceptual and later bureaucratic, upon a world alien to them. The suffix "ism" implies a doctrinal system, a unity of thought, which was not found among the diverse religious practices of the subcontinent. Taken together, these three ideas—Manu's textual approach to caste, the misapplication of the Muslim geographic perception, and the pseudo-system implied in the British concept of "Hinduism"— have coalesced to present the commonsense view of the caste system as a uniquely Hindu phenomenon.

To look for an overarching Hindu ideological basis for caste is thus to look in the wrong place. India's religious and caste practices are local in character. No overarching sacralization need be sought to explain cultural assumptions about "the differentiation of all living being into general groups . . . each of which possesses a defining code of conduct carried in its bodily substance" ("Caste", 1987:4). Once the pseudo-issue of "Hindu" sacralization is set aside, it becomes much easier to account for the obvious fact of caste formation among non-Hindu groups, something which would otherwise remain puzzling or eccentric at best.

The Cochin Jews, who have adopted many Hindu practices, have yet scrupulously ensured that their syncretic religious patterns do not violate Jewish legal or ethical principles. In so doing they have done what Jews everywhere have done: They have maintained a distinct identity while adapting creatively into their cultural milieu. The Cochin Jews' adaptation to their Indian environment is evidenced in their proliferation into four endogamous subcastes,[6]

---

[6]The Cochin Jews' emulation of caste behavior in dividing themselves into four endogamous subcastes was the one instance in which their adaptation of

their ritual use of Hebrew paralleling Hindu use of Sanskrit, their rigorous observance of the dietary restrictions of *Kashruth*; and their removal of footwear in the synagogue. Some of their practices—such as endogamy, the use of a sacred language, adherence to dietary codes, and concern for family purity, entailing avoidance of menstruating women—represent points at which Jewish and Hindu values converge. Other practices point to more specific borrowings.

A number of the Cochin Jews' practices appear to have been borrowed from the highest Kerala Brahman caste, the Nambudiris. For example, the various Jew Towns of Kerala were designed in a similar manner to the Brahman towns. Perhaps more significant are similarities in the economic organization of the communities. In each case, individuals were dependent upon the synagogue or temple, which possessed vast estates. The Jews also resemble the Nambudiris in their emphasis upon purity of descent (*yichus*); in their close association with the Cheraman Perumal emperors of Cranganore (Johnson, 1986:164-165); in their relatively fair complexion and the importance attributed to their foreign origin (*yichus* from ancient Israel); in the use of a series of paintings in the synagogue or temple to narrate the community's "sacred history" (Johnson, 1986:162); and in the custom that "only women and men of the higher castes were allowed to cover the upper part of their bodies . . ." (Johnson, 1985:170).

The Cochin Jews have also had close links with the Nayars, politically and economically the dominant caste in Kerala. The Jews established not only very cordial and fond relations with the Nayar maharajas, but also an intricate system of mutual dependence. The Jews enjoyed the hospitality and protection of the maharajas, and it was by royal invitation that the Cochin Synagogue was built beside the palace and royal temple. On the one hand, the Jews provided the maharajas not only with their best soldiers, but

Hindu patterns clashed with *halachic* ethical norms. On this unsavory aspect of Cochin Jewish history, see our article, "Jewish Apartheid and a Jewish Gandhi," *Jewish Social Studies* 1988/1993: 147-176.

were also their contacts with the world beyond Kerala's shores. Being part of an international people with commerical interests spanning the globe, the Jews were traders, interpreters, and diplomats in the service of the maharajas. Much of the legendary wealth of Cochin was due to its relatively advanced position in such trade, which was managed for the most part by such Jewish leaders as the House of Rahabi. Such proximity with a high caste of course tends to "rub off", and in many aspects of their behavior the Cochin Jews resemble the Nayars as well.

For example, the social prestige and independence enjoyed by the women in Jew Town in part reflects the Jewish community's contact with the matrilineal Nayars. Once a "primary marriage" had been contracted with a Nambudiri man, Nayar women traditionally enjoyed autonomy in selecting sexual partners. While Jewish women's sexuality is strictly limited, their autonomy is more generalized and is most evident in their participation in religious education and, later, professional achievement. In day-to-day interactions, women and men are strikingly equal, and this equality could not be attributed to that associated with modernization because it predates and in some respects exceeds it.

A similarity between Jewish and Nayar marriage customs has also been observed: "Jewish law permits both cross-cousin and parallel-cousin marriages, unlike many South Indian groups which encourage cross-cousin but prohibit parallel-cousin alliances. The Nayars of Central Kerala permit both" (Johnson, 1985:427, n.2). Another, rather trifling borrowing from the Nayars is the Jewish women's custom of wearing a tiger's claw set in gold as a talisman (Johnson, 1985:171).

Examples of parallels between the Jews and the Nambudiris and the Nayars could be extended, all of which would count as evidence of an "attributional" approach to the study of caste, in which "a caste's rank derives from the characteristics of its way of life, high or low according to the criteria of collective purity" (Dumont, 1980:90). However, when discussing the Cochin Jews' place in the caste system, an "interactional" approach to caste must be taken into consideration as well. By this method, "castes are ranked according to the structure of interaction among them . . . [especially in] the ritualized giving and receiving of food. . . . Emphasis in this system of ranking is not on qualities, but on transactions." (Marriott, 1959:96-97).

The Cochin Jews have secured a high place for themselves in the caste hierarchy by adopting aspects of the life-style and practices of the two highest castes in Kerala. The complex dynamics of this process of appropriation is clearly evident in the ritual observances associated with the festivals of Passover and Simchat Torah which, as we shall see, involve the creative adaptation of the symbols of the Nambudiri Brahmans and of the Nayars, respectively. The Passover observances of the Cochin Jews also provide an example of the way in which ritualized exchanges of food determine a group's relative status in the hierarchy.

Passover and Priestly-Ascetic Symbols of Purity

In virtually every country in which they have lived, Jews have adopted "additional observances" (*hiddur mitzvot*) to those required by *halacha*, "which express the Jew's love of the *mitzvot* by embellishing them..." (Chill, 1979:xx). Passover preparations in Cochin are striking in this regard. In certain ways they are more fastidious than those found in other Jewish communities, even the most orthodox. The question arises, why do the Cochin Jews exaggerate their Passover observances? Why do they embellish them with additional observances?

The answer is complex, and it involves the value attached to purity and ascetic behavior in Hindu society. It is in emulation of the Brahman priests' concern with purity that Jews have based their own parallel traditions, and nowhere in Jewish tradition is purity more emphasized than in a disdain that borders on the obsessive for leavening (*chamets*) and that which might come into contact with leavening prior to and during the eight-day Passover festival. The fine balance that the Cochin Jews have maintained between the worlds of Judaism and Hinduism is evident in their Passover observances, in which a form of asceticism that has served to integrate them into Kerala's caste system has been added to norma-tive Jewish practice. In addition to its usual Jewish meanings—a celebration of the Exodus story, a commemoration of Temple sacrifices, and a springtime agricultural festival—Cochin's Pass-over observances add another layer of meaning. This additional meaning, which takes the form of exemplary group asceticism and a period of liminal separation from the non-Jewish world, is the reassertion of the group's high caste status.

Victor Turner (1977) holds that a marginal position affords fresh and enlivening perspectives on familiar structures. The Cochin Jews have been marginal in India in several senses—as India's most microscopic minority, as a cultural and commerical bridge between East and West, and as a subject of study at the interstices between the usual academic disciplines. They are doubly marginal as Jews in the context of India and as Indians in the context of world Jewry, and their marginality affords an occasion to look with fresh eyes at such familiar institutions as Passover and asceticism.

With respect to Passover, the interstitial position of the Cochin Jews forces us to reconsider the meanings usually associated with its observance. The austerity of Passover celebrations that we observed in Cochin, where it is known as "the fasting feast", were striking. What is unambiguously joyous and intergenerational elsewhere was in Cochin relatively somber, with no special roles for children. Women worked to the point of exhaustion, purity was stressed as nowhere else in the Jewish world, the usual warm relationships with non-Jews were held in abeyance for the eight days of the festival, there was no raucous ransoming of the *afiqoman*[7]

---

[7]The Seder plate contains, among other symbolic foods, unleavened bread, *matsah*. While there were once two pieces of *matsah* on the Seder plate (Maimonides, 1988:160), it has become customary to have three, representing the division of the Jewish people into the *Kohanim* or priests, the *Leviyim* or scribes, and the Israelites, or commoners. (There are other explanations for the three pieces of *matsah*, see Schneerson, 1985:6-7). The term *afiqoman*, Greek for "dessert", is applied to half of the middle *matsah*, broken off, wrapped, and set aside. It is required to conclude the Seder meal with this *afiqoman* (Maimonides, 1988:166-167; cf. Schneerson, 1985:53). In Ashkenazi custom, the children "steal" the *afiqoman*, and the father (or whoever conducts the Seder) must pay a ransom to get

at the Seder (ritual meal), and children did not ask the traditional four questions, which were instead chanted in unison. The mood of "Pesah work" was frantic, and of the Seder, subdued. Of course the usual symbols were on the Seder table, and the Passover text, the *Haggadah*, was identical to that elsewhere. However, the mood was quite different.

The ascetic nature of Passover observances in Jew Town also forces us to reconsider the nature of asceticism itself and to question whether treatments of the subject have not been overly spiritualized. By exclusive concern with asceticism's spiritual orientation, have we perhaps failed to recognize its very down-to-earth meanings and rewards? Scholarship on asceticism generally revolves around two issues: (1) the ideational framework for asceticism, which treats motives and purported rewards for ascetic practices, and (2) forms of ascetic practices. Each of these issues must be considered separately. The data from Cochin pose no quarrel with asceticism's forms, but rigorously challenge what is understood as its "ideology".

Virtually all studies of asceticism echo the longstanding view of T. C. Hall: "Primarily asceticism consists in the contradiction of natural desires under the mandate of some higher, or supposed higher, ideal set by the will before the life" (1958:63). In the interval between Hall's entry in James Hastings' classic *Encyclopaedia of Religion and Ethics* and the contemporary *Encyclopaedia of Religion* edited by Mircea Eliade, there has apparently been no devel-

---

it back. Alternately, the father hides the *afiqoman*, offering a price to the child who finds it. The absence of specific roles for children at the Cochini Seder is striking. The four questions, the starting-point for the recitation of the narrative, elsewhere are asked by the youngest son. Maimonides (1988:132-136) even recommended ruses, such as snatching away the *matsah*, to spark youthful curiosity. In Cochin the four questions, indeed the entire *Haggadah*, were chanted in unison. Also, there was no cup of wine for the harbinger of the Messiah, Eliahu Hanabi. Interpreting these aspects of the Cochin *minhag* is risky. Nevertheless, it was intriguing that both customs truncate those themes in the Seder most closely associated with redemption: children and Eliahu. Could it be that the ease and security of life in India made redemption a less pressing issue than it was in less hospitable regions of exile?

opment in thinking about asceticism. In the latter work Walter O. Kaelber defines asceticism "as a voluntary, sustained, and at least partially systematic program of self-discipline and self-denial in which immediate, sensual, or profane gratifications are renounced in order to obtain a higher spiritual state or a more thorough absorption in the sacred" (1987:44).

Variants of these definitions could be enumerated without end. The point under consideration is the goal for which asceticism is understood to be practised: a highly spiritualized, other-worldly goal. Whether this goal is conceived as Kaelber's "absorption in the sacred", or Rosemary Rader's "initiation or maintenance of contact with divinity, or some supranatural or transcendent being" (1987:286), all asceticism is believed to have "a moral purport, and is based on the eternal contrast of the proposition, 'This is right,' with the proposition, 'That is pleasant.' " ("Asceticism", 1910:11, 717).

While no one would deny that very high spiritual motives such as "absorption in the sacred" are often involved in ascetic practices, it seems that insisting upon any unidimensional goal for asceticism does not do justice to the complexity, nuance, and overdetermination of human motivation and behavior. In religious studies in particular, one must guard against simple, univocal answers. What our observations of Passover in Cochin demand is recognition that status is also a very important motive in religious behavior. Moreover, what immediately becomes apparent from this observation is that it is by no means unique to the Cochin Jews. Status is an equally important motivating force in the ascetic life of the Hindu *sadhu*, the Buddhist *bhikshu*, the village *Brahman*, and the Jain layman.

The forms of asceticism according to Kaelber are : "(1) fasting, (2) sexual continence, (3) poverty, under which may be included begging, (4) seclusion or isolation, and (5) self-inflicted pain, either physical ... or mental." (1987:422). The Cochin Passover practices that we observed involved all but sexual continence, and fasting and isolation were primary. Fasting generally involves either total abstention from all food or partial abstention from particular foods (Rader, 1987:289). In Cochin the fast was partial. With respect to isolation, it is often an individual ascetic who is secluded, in accordance with the hermit ideal. However, a group may undergo a period of temporary liminal seclusion that often precedes rituals of status elevation (Turner, 1977). In Cochin, where caste status is an integral component of Passover rituals, the community as a whole became isolated from its normal context prior to and during the festival. As we shall see, this isolation was a crucial component for the ritual establishment and celebration of their status in the context of Hindu Kerala.

Passover practices throughout the Jewish world, of course, involve a modified fast in the abstention from leaven and that which might have come into contact with leaven, or *chamets*—pronounced *hamas* in the sweet-sounding Hebrew of Cochin. Fasting is often connected with purity, purification, and pollution, as is the avoidance of *chamets*, which is the origin of spring-cleaning associated with Easter in Christian communities and simply with springtime among secularists. However, Cochin *minhag*—especially with regard to cleaning, separation, and purity—went beyond standard *halachic* requirements to a marked degree and in uniquely Indian ways. This excess can be traced to the dynamic interplay of asceticism, diet, and caste in Kerala, and the need for the Cochin Jews, as "foreign" meat-eaters in a society that valorizes vegetarianism to reassert periodically their high caste status.

According to *halacha*, preparations for Pesach, pronounced Pesah in Cochin, should begin thirty days before the festival (Zalman 1985:3, 1; cf. Fredman, 1981:12-13; Berman, 1982:148), which is to say that they should begin just after Purim. In Cochin, however, the Chanukah candles had barely cooled before "Pesah work", as it is called, began to warm up. First came the cleaning of the tea, chilies, tamarind, and spices to be set aside for Passover use. "Now the work for Pesah begins," Sarah Cohen said on January 15th, when she bought a basket of tamarind for Passover cleaning. "Everything must start afresh for Pesah", shd added, combining the motifs of special preparations and cleaning with the traditional understanding of Pesach as a "second new year", coming as it does during the first month of the Jewish lunar calendar.

"Pesah work" increasingly dominated life in Jew Town from the beginning of the month of Teveth until the middle of Nisan— about one hundred days. So important was "Pesah work" to the Cochin community that they believed that if the women made even the slightest mistake in Passover preparations, the lives of their husbands and children would be endangered. As Jacob Cohen explained, "The legend is that they won't make it to the next Pesah. That's why women are more orthodox than men."

Special rooms for storing Passover items were scrubbed, followed by all utensils, pots, and crockery. Houses were painted or whitewashed soon after Purim, a custom not found elsewhere, except among the Beta Yisra'el Jews of Ethiopia and among some Yemeni Jews. This *minhag* reflects the Hindu custom of whitewashing homes in preparation for the Holi festival. Yet whatever was done in 1987 paled in comparison with observance in days gone by. Sarah Cohen recollected, "The elders would scrape off all paint from the previous year, using coconut fiber, and then repaint everything. They say *hamas* would be there, too, so they would scrape it off."

Wells were drained and scrubbed, lest they be polluted by a crumb of bread (Ganzfried, 1961:3, 43). Each grain of rice to be used during the festival had to be examined to ensure that it was free from defects, or cracks into which polluting *chamets* might have found its way, after which it was known as "Pesah rice". Cushion covers and curtains were replaced with special ones for the holiday. Wooden furniture was stripped and re-polished. Many of these observances have been documented in Barbara C. Johnson's doctoral dissertation (1985), and all of them evidence the traditional Jewish concern for avoiding any contact with *chamets*, carried to a remarkable degree of fastidiousness.

Making wine—either the fermented *yayin* or the fresh *mai*[8]— was a major undertaking in Jew Town, and represents an instance

---

[8]*Yayin*, Hebrew for wine, was made from fresh grapes and sugar sealed in a container and stirred daily for twelve days, then strained and bottled. The word *mai* is of unknown etymology, although it might have derived from the Hebrew *mayim*, water. It was simply grape juice which was strained through cheese cloth.

in which *halachic* and Cochini concerns for purity perfectly over-lapped. Judaism's abhorrence of idolatry manifests itself in severe restrictions about wine. As wine was used to consecrate pagan idols, any wine that might be so used is forbidden to Jews. Therefore, only wine made by Jews is considered *kosher*. However, the restrictions have come to resemble Hindu taboos about food preparation when taken to an extreme: if this Jewish-made wine is touched by a Gentile, it becomes forbidden because, as *halacha* assumes the Gentile to be religious, he or she is likely to dedicate some of the wine to the gods (Zalman, 1985:2, 53-107, 504ff; cf. Cohen, 1970:128). The Cochin Jews went one step further: if even the shelf or table upon which the wine sat were touched by a Gentile servant, the wine became taboo.

Similar scrupulous restrictions govern *matsah*, pronounced *massa* in Cochin. Many hours are spent inspecting each grain of wheat for cracks or breaks that might indicate leavening due to contact with water or into which *chamets* might have become embedded. This inspection is performed three times: first by non-Jewish servants, then twice by Jewish women (or, rarely, a Jewish man). Once the third inspection takes place and all broken grains are removed, neither the wheat nor its containers nor the shelf on which it rests can be touched by non-Jews. As with the wine preparations, it is this extra prohibition that marks off Cochin observance from *halachic* norms.

Grinding the wheat was traditionally performed at home, but in recent times the diminished number of Jews in Cochin has led to some modifications. In 1987 wheat was ground in the nearby, Hindu-owned Kanchana Flour Mill, which had been specially cleaned the previous evening by the compliant proprietor. Jewish women brought the wheat early the next morning and then perfomed a second cleaning of the milling machinery. To ensure that there was no contact between the wheat and non-Jews, the miller touched only the machinery. It was the women who poured in the wheat kernels and collected the flour, which was then returned to Jew Town for sifting.

The climax of "Pesah work" was "*massa* day". Early on that day the women and young people gathered in the courtyard of Queenie Hallegua's vast home. The only jobs that could be performed by Gentile servants were the tending of the fire of coconut husks (charcoal was mixed with the husks as an innovation in 1987), which heated the flat iron griddles, and the scouring of special mixing bowls called *legen* with "a bit of clean new coconut fiber and the soapy substance from a small green soapnut fruit, which the Jews use only for Passover washing, because it is thought to be particularly pure" (Johnson, 1985:237).

Water, which had been drawn from a purified well and cooled by standing overnight in special earthenware jugs kept solely for this purpose, was used to knead the flour (see Zalman, 1985:3-4, 1025). The *massa* was then rolled out using *kozhali*, hollow brass cylinders filled with metal beads, which were used only for this purpose and which produced a sweet, bell-like sound. Blessings were said over each household's batch of flour, usually around two kilograms, and the obligatory *chalah* (the portion of the dough that during Temple days is set aside for the *kohanim*) was thrown into the fire. The whole process used to be accompanied by the sounding of the *shofar* and the chanting of Passover songs and sections from the *Haggadah*.

It is generally accepted that the purity associated with the *kohanim*, or hereditary priests in the Temple cult, was later transferred to all of Israel as "a nation of priests", especially but not exclusively regarding the *kashruth* system of food purity (Neusner, 1973:66-67). The table in every home replaced the public Temple. Jewish restrictions about food are in many ways analogous to the Brahman's restrictions concerning food purity, and such restrictions are identity markers for both groups. The methods of preparation of "emblematic" foods in Cochin during the partial fast of Passover—*massa* in particular, but wine and other consumables as well—exceed *halachic* norms at crucial points, many of which resemble high-caste Hindu taboos about possible pollution by contact with *pakka* (cooked) food. As Yosef Hallegua put it, "Pesah is the *cleanest* holiday".

Jokes and complaints tended to reinforce the ascetic quality of

Passover preparations and observances in Cochin. Recalling that the ascetic's self-infliction of pain may be psychological as well as physical, such banter should not be thought of as insignificant. Despite dinner tables laden with steaming biriyanis and curries, the meals were said to be too meagre to sustain life—"the fasting feast" theme. "Bread fills up the holes in a diet," complained Jacob Cohen. Gamliel Salem, the community's most unabashed skeptic, joked, "Just because Moses did these things so long ago, we all have to suffer now. What rotten nonsense!" Meals at the Brahman-run Krishna Cafe were often recalled with an exaggerated fondness. As we shall see, this particular form of banter that opposed Brahman (or Jain) food with Jewish food during Passover was closely connected with the status that is associated with food exchange in India.

Seclusion and isolation are common ascetic practices, and there was an intriguing variant of this form among the Cochin Jews. By nature gregarious, they became increasingly isolated from their non-Jewish friends during the month or two prior to Passover, culminating in an almost total isolation during the eight days of the festival itself losing, for a while, their usual connectedness with their Hindu neighbors.

During 1987 Passover coincided with the local Hindu festival, Vishu. Sarah Cohen complained, with a real feeling of loss, "It's too bad that Vishu falls during our Pesah this year. Otherwise we would all go to the [Hindu] temple and mix with our Hindu friends and take our lunch with them."

Their gradual and increasing isolation became apparent by the festival of Purim, one month before Passover, by which time "Pesah work" had become so dominating and consuming that there was little time for interactions outside of the community. Cochin Jews generally enjoy sharing food and conversation with their Hindu, Christian, Jain, Muslim, and Parsi friends on any occasion. In fact, the intercommunal exchange of special foods, such as special cakes for the Jewish new year, Rosh Hashanah, is particulary enjoyed— but not during Passover.

The Cochin Jews believed that the only way to ensure the avoidance of *chamets* was to avoid their non-Jewish friends. "For eight days I cut off everything. If I see my friends," Isaac Askhenazy said, "they may offer a cup of tea or some food. Actually, Pesah is a very hard time for us." Sarah Cohen warned, "Don't go outside [of Jew Town]. You might make a mistake and eat or drink something you can't have." While they would have enjoyed a visit with friends or to the local Brahman restaurant, the Krishna Cafe, such visits were scrupulously avoided: "The main thing," according to Reema Salem, "is that we take nothing from outside." During the Passover festival, the universe of the Cochin Jews did not extend beyond Synagogue Lane.

Their avoidance of *chamets* thus translated into the temporary avoidance of non-Jews. Only one family regularly invited "outsiders" to their Seder: Sattu and Gladys Koder, the leaders of the community, have traditionally borne the responsibility for the group's external relations. It is believed that the presence of a non-Jew at the Seder table "pollutes" the ritual (cf. Schneerson, 1985:43, n.a). This exclusion was so contrary to the group's usual gregarious instincts that a compromise had on occasion been effected by aligning two dining tables under one table cloth, so that the ritual separation of tables was maintained while being kept, quite literally, under cover so as not to offend their Gentile guests (Johnson, 1985:163).

A celebratory reaggregation into Kerala society culminated this period, which resembles the liminal phase observed in African coming-of-age rites by Victor Turner (1977). The liminality that had temporarily suspended normal societal interactions, which are of necessity hierarchical in Kerala, led to a reaffirmation of that hierarchy after a ritualized reaggregation in the form of a charming *"hamas party"* hosted by a neighbor, D.B. Khona, an influential Jain businessman who was also the lay leader of the local Jain temple. Thus the ritually bounded separation and isolation of the Cochin Jews were both temporary and communal.

The more obvious instances of ascetic, self-inflicted pain used to be performed just prior to Yom Kippur. Nevertheless, as mentioned earlier, there was also a degree of self-inflicted pain involved in the Passover of Cochin, although this pain was more psychological than physcial—at least for the men. Passover was anticipated with dread. Cochin men bemoaned Passover as "the fasting feast" and "a nuisance festival" when there was "*nothing* to eat". Interestingly, leaven became overvalued prior to and during Passover. Protestations of a need for "a cold beer"—something only rarely drunk in this community—were repeatedly made. Discussions of what desired foods were forbidden increased as Passover drew nearer, often accompanied by vigorous protests. The fact that all of these complaints were made half in jest did not diminish their psychological effect.

The women, who had to ready their large homes for the festival, suffered more, their pain exacerbated by the terribly hot weather of the pre-monsoon months. For example, the temperature on *massa* day 1987 was 1020 and the humidity was high; in the baking area it must have surpassed 1200. Bodily perspiration quite literally boiled off, causing painful skin burns. The very real pain associated with "Pesah work" was verbally reinforced: "Cleaning the wheat, a backbreaking job," said Sarah Cohen. Summing up, she added, "During Pesah you die from the work, and then there is no food to eat!"

While poverty as such is not a virtue in Judaism, it should be noted that the Cochin Jews went to a great deal of expense in the annual repainting or whitewashing of their large homes, in hiring workers to drain and scrub their wells and water tanks, and in the stripping and re-polishing of their furniture. Painting a large house cost between six and seven thousand rupees (that is, more than US $500), while employing casual workers to clean their wells cost at least sixty rupees ($5). They willingly undertook these expensive practices, which many of them could not afford.

Four of the five general forms of asceticism were found in the Cochin Passover: fasting, in the modified form of avoidance of leaven, which went beyond the requirements of normative Judaism; a temporary isolation of the community from non-Jewish Cochin, a period of separation reminiscent of Turner's paradigm of liminality; self-inflicted psychological and perhaps even physical pain; and a degree of expense that caused real financial difficulties for many in

the community. Absent from among these forms was sexual abstinence, or at least this was not observed to have been the case.

Despite the ascetic character of Passover observances, the
festival brought with it its own humor in the form of offhanded
comments that reflected very serious issues such as the community's
place in the larger society of Cochin. And place, as Jonathan Z.
Smith reminds us, is to be understood "not simply in the sense of
environmental generation, but also in the sense of social location,
of genealogy, kinship, authority, superordination, and subordina-
tion" (1987:46).

One example of the serious implications of Passover humor can
be seen in the Cochin Jews' exaggerated longing for a snack at the
Krishna Cafe. In India, and the South in particular, one finds
Brahman-run restaurants in every town. The dietary rule of thumb
is that "the cook must be as pure as the eater" (Dumont, 1980:139),
so one implicitly acknowledges another's equal or greater purity by
the simple act of taking food from him or her. Brahmans have the
strictest dietary regulations of any caste in India, except for the
Jains. The fact that anyone can eat food cooked by a Brahman
indicates the Brahmans' high status.

To joke about missing a Krishna Cafe meal was to point out that,
for the duration of Passover at least, even this pure Brahman food
was not pure enough. The special requirements for avoiding *chamets*
during Passover added a layer of food taboos that *ipso facto* carried
a high status. As succinctly put by Dumont, "superiority and
superior purity are identical" (1980:56). This drama of purity and
status was played out nightly in Jew Town, and provided an
example of the "interactional" basis of caste ranking discussed
earlier, in which castes are ranked according to the structure of their
transactions, especially those involved in the ritualized giving and
receiving of food.

On a typical week night in Jew Town, a car pulled up to Elias
Koder's house at 7:30 p.m. sharp, as it had done for more than
fifteen years. The car belonged to D.B. Khona, a Jain businessman
whom everyone called "Bapusait", who proceeded to carry his
usual array of stainless steel tiffin carriers filled with snacks into

Elias's house. A few minutes later Koder's Jewish neighbors, Jacob Cohen and I.C. Hallegua, strolled in. Dr. Panikar, a Hindu surgeon, was usually last, coming directly from a nearby hospital. Occasionally V.K. Hamza, a Muslim lawyer, also dropped in, as did P.M. Jussay, a Syrian Christian newspaper editor, to complete the scene. With all "members" assembled, having taken their places around a huge table, the drinking club came to order.

A teetotaler hiself, Koder nonetheless made sure there was plenty of rum, whiskey, and mixers to go around. And it literally did, on a lazy Susan that seemed to be in perpetual motion as the men reached for refreshments. As the drinks continued to flow, so did the conversation. There was talk of business, politics, risque jokes, gossip, and quite often, religious matters.

Bapusait played the role of the provider for the group because as a Jain he was subject to the most stringent dietary regulations of anyone, beyond even the Brahmans. Whatever came from his kitchen was pure enough for anyone. However, it seemed that what was at stake, more than such reasoned practicality, was the issue of who provided the food.

Given the Jews' isolation from the non-Jewish world during Passover, one might have expected the drinking club to be suspended during the festival. It was not, however, and an analysis reveals the symbolic importance of maintaining the club's nightly meetings during this period.

As Passover drew closer the conversation more and more turned to the festival's dietary requirements. Whiskey and beer could not be taken, of course. Brandy was considered acceptable because it was made from grapes rather than a suspicious grain. Discussion ensued. Indian brandy was also a grain product, flavored to resemble its European model, and technically should have been avoided. Samuel Hallegua suggested that they drink only French cognac during Passover, an idea that was lauded until someone mentioned the exorbitant price that a bottle of imported brandy fetched on the Ernakulam black market (more than US $50). Despite religious scruples, it was decided to make do with the Indian variety of brandy.

As the discussion turned from drinks to snacks, Bapusait became especially curious. "Could you eat parched corn? How about flat rice pancakes?" When he learned that flat rice pancakes would be acceptable, he quickly offered to bring them. "No, because we don't know what else is in your kitchen, what has been cooked in your pots, where *hamas* could be found," Jacob Cohen replied.

However, Bapusait was undaunted: "I will buy new pots to cook your pancakes and will only carry them on new plates. Could you eat them then?" At this point the conversation broke down into laughter. "We just can't take anything from outside," the Jews said, and Bapusait was crestfallen. Eventually he satisfied himself with bringing delicious mangoes (Passover falls during the mango season in Kerala), as fresh fruit is in any case *kosher le-Pesach.*

The fact that the discussion was enjoyed by all did not diminish its significance: by "out-Brahmaning the Brahman", the Jews' status during this period of liminality was established. Even the purest Jain food was not pure enough, at least temporarily.

Passover celebrations culminated at Elias's house in "*hamas* party" hosted by Bapusait. He brought *iddlis, puris,* sweetmeats, and other temporarily forbidden treats. The Jews especially relished the *chamets*—Gamliel Salem had been yearning "to eat *hamas* like hell" for days—thereby ending their liminal period of abstinence from certain foods and from contact with their non-Jewish friends. At the same time Bapusait resumed his role as provider, ritually reintegrating the Jews into the larger, hierarchical Kerala society. The Jews' high status thus ritually re-established, they returned to and reaffirmed the society in which they had lived so happily for so long.

Simchat Torah and the Noble Symbols of Royalty

Every spring in the ritual observances of the Passover festival, the Cochin Jews reassert their high place in the caste hierarchy by demonstrating their purity in accordance with the Brahmanical-ascetic structure. Every autumn, on the other hand, in the ritual enactments of the High Holy Days, and in particular Simchat Torah, they give precedence to a different set of symbols, symbols of royalty and wealth, in accordance with the Kshatriya noble power structures represented in Kerala by the Nayars.

This emphasis on symbols of royalty represents a natural extension of the liturgical theme of the autumn High Holy Days, which celebrates God's kingship (*malchut* in Hebrew). One of the most popular prayers, unique to the season, is *Avinu Malchenu*, "Our Father, Our King". Beginning with the morning service on Rosh Hashanah and continuing through Yom Kippur, it is God's attribute of royalty or nobility that is the focus of the prayers. In Cochin indigenous songs enhance this symbolism, as do the unique manner of displaying Torah scrolls and the joyous afternoon processions on Simchat Torah. Royalty, one of the two symbolic complexes by which the Jews' place in Kerala society has been ritually established and celebrated, is the *leitmotif* of the autumn holy days.

Concluding the fall cycle of holy days is the two-day festival known in Cochin as Shmini. Most synagogues in the West observe two separate festivals, Shmini Chag Atzeret and Simchat Torah. In Israel Shmini Chag Atzeret and Simchat Torah are celebrated together in one day, the second festival day being a Diaspora observance. Shmini Chag Atzeret commemorates the additional sacrifices offered after Sukkot at the Temple, and Simchat Torah is a non-Biblical celebration of the conclusion of the yearly cycle of Torah reading and the beginning of the new cycle (Chill, 1979:236). In Cochin Shmini is of enormous significance, arguably the community's most distinctive autumn observance.

For the Shmini celebration that we observed the Cochin Jews dressed in their finest and shiniest clothes. Strolling up Synagogue Lane for evening prayers, we were confronted by a "tree of light"—a twelve foot metal "tree" whose branches supported blazing oil lamps. The Jews were quick to remind their guests that, in days gone by, there were "trees" before each of Synagogue Lane's three synagogues. At the base of the clock tower was a similar contraption in the shape of a Star of David. The overall effect was dazzling. It was evident that Shmini in Cochin was to be very, very special.

The festive air outside the synagogue paled in comparison with the splendor inside. The synagogue, brilliant and colorful at any time, was utterly dazzling on Shmini. The whitewashed walls and dark wooden benches were covered with golden satin. The effect of the shimmering walls reflecting the blazing oil lamps encircling the *tebah* (pulpit) suffused the dainty prayer hall with a light that bordered on the supernal. All around the upper half of the walls were *parochets*, "curtains" made of deceased Cochini women's festive sarongs, in green, gold, blue, red, and white embroidered silks. The impact was enhanced by an olfactory stimulus as well: hanging among the many chandeliers and oil lamps were string upon string of freshly plucked jasmine flowers.

The most striking decorations transformed the aron *hakodesh* (holy ark). A special temporary ark had been constructed between two tall silver pillars. The platform was covered with red, gold-embroidered Banarsi silk. All seven Torah scrolls, replete with gold, jewel-encrusted crowns and silver *rimomim* (finials), were proudly displayed. The effect was completed by a canopy of red and gold silks, topped off with the lid of the synagogue's famous solid gold *kiddush* cup, the one that had been used to break the fast of Kippur a fortnight before and that had sanctified every bride and bridegroom in Cochin for centuries.

The synagogue had become a vision of eternity.

Simchat Torah prayers increased in intensity through each of the festival's three services, those on the first evening being the most subdued. The synagogue was crowded for *Arbith* (evening) services. Jews from as far away as Bombay, Trivandrum, and Madras, not to mention Ernakulam and Alwaye, were present, as well as Jewish travellers from Switzerland, South Africa, England, Israel, and America. As the seven *haqafot* (circumambulations around the *tebah* with the Torah scrolls) commenced, songbooks were produced and the synagogue was filled with haunting Shingly tunes, melodies composed centuries earlier in the Cochin Jews' ancestral home of Cranganore. Bottles of rum, brandy, and whiskey began to appear in the corners and recesses of the building—as well as in the women's section—and dancing, jumping, and clapping accompanied the singing.

By *Shacharit* prayers the next morning, the mood had become even more festive. The high spirits were enhanced by the "petrol" drunk to lighten the steps of the younger men, who carried the Torah scrolls, as well as the voices of the older men and the women, who were the chanters. As the men caught their breath after each circumambulation of the *tebah* with the heavy, metal-encased scrolls elaborately bedecked with crowns and *rimomim*, a fellow celebrant would invariably tap one of the men's shoulders, a naughty grin on his lips, and invite him to share "Petrol! Petrol!" The scroll would be passed to other eager arms, and the two would disappear in the crowded apartment of the *shamash*, the caretaker, adjacent to the synagogue. On the dining table were bottle after bottle of liquor, as well as boiled potatoes and eggs to ease the absorption of the spirits. Half a potato and a healthy shot of brandy later, the reveler would be back in the procession, singing *shir'ot* (songs) more loudly than ever and, quite literally, jumping with delight.

Apart from the seven *haqafot*, the focus of the morning prayers was reading from the Sefer Torah. On this festival the very lines of the Torah about the death of Moses were followed immediately by the very first lines, which describe the creation of the world, *Bereshit*. Symbolically, every Jew is wedded to the Torah, and the one who reads the concluding verses of *Devarim* (Deuteronomy) is traditionally called *Chatan Torah,* the bridegroom of the Torah. The one who reads the first lines is called *Chatan Bereshit*, bridegroom of Genesis, and in the Cochin *minhag* should be the most recent groom among the community. Bridegrooms, like the festival itself, partake of the symbolism of nobility.

The *Haftarah* (prophetic reading) for Simchat Torah was sung in Shingly cantillation and pronunciation, as were its blessings—an especially beautiful chant. The popular Sephardi songs, *Imre na* and *Mi spharad hikachti* were also chanted with Shingly

melodies. Shingly or Cranganore was the site of Indian Jewish
sovereignty, the home of the archetypal Jewish prince, Joseph
Rabban. The use of Shingly cantillation and pronunciation thus
linked the festival with Jewish nobility.

The three afternoon *haqafot* in the courtyard, outside of the
synagogue building, are unique among Jews throughout the world
(S.H.Hallegua, 1986:6). A red coir carpet was laid around the
synagogue. The younger and stronger men carried the scrolls while
older men sprinkled rose water on them. There were worries
whether there were enough able-bodied young men to complete
the circumambulations with the heavy scrolls, while in days gone
by the concern was whether there would be enough rounds to give
everyone a chance to carry the beloved scrolls. Mandelbaum, in
his earlier study of the Cochin Jews, observed the children's eager
participation:

> The younger men try hard to have the honor of carrying them.
> There are two small scrolls which are carried by boys. I noticed
> one little fellow tearfully pleading with his father that he might
> have the privilege of bearing the *sefer*. The privilege must be
> purchased, and when the father finally nodded his assent, the
> boy went bounding off in an about face of emotion, to tell his
> friends of his luck (1939:458).

Men, women and children all lustily chanted the unique
Cochini Hebrew songs proclaiming their love of Torah. The entire
liturgy for the afternoon *haqafot* was composed in Cranganore,
according to local tradition. The older men led the processions,
walking backwards as they sang, facing the scrolls, carrying
handwritten songbooks. The women, dressed in brilliant saris and
kerchiefs, sang no less enthusiastically. This festival was the only
time women freely entered the main hall of the synagogue.

After the *haqafot* the synagogue emptied as everyone headed
home for a rest. Almost everyone. During the 1930s Cecil Koder
introduced yet another festivity to Simchat Torah observances:
water fights. Reminiscent of the riotous Hindu festival Holi,

Synagogue Lane on Simchat Torah afternoon became a mock battleground. Pails of water were poured over any and every unsuspecting head, followed by a recent addition: rotten eggs, which had been hidden away and painted with Hebrew festive greetings. Some elders scurried to bar their doors, but most accepted a rotten egg and pail of water as their due. In any event, there was time for a shower before Mincha prayers. Mandelbaum aptly commented upon the seemingly chaotic merriment:

> On this day the tears in the social fabric are mended. All quarrels are supposed to be patched up on Simchat Torah, and many dissentions really are smoothed over in the general merry-making. The least of the congregation enjoys the honor of reading the blessings before the Law together with the most distinguished. Women are allowed to come into the synagogue hall to kiss the sacred books. At noon the young people dine in houses other than their own. Wine and arrack flow copiously and some men become gloriously tight. Like drunken men the world over, they crack muddled jokes and bawl out catchy tunes. But in Cochin the tunes that they sing in their groggy animation are synagogue melodies, hymns and paeans to the Lord of Israel (1939:457-458).

After taking a rest, the Jews returned to the synagogue for *Mincha* (afternoon) prayers at 6:30 p.m. The Cochin Simchat Torah *Mincha* is a unique and highly significant service. Its importance in the community is clear. When Yaakob Daniel Cohen established a Hebrew-Malayalam printing press in Jew Town in 1877, his very first publication was a liturgy for this occasion (*Seder Mincha Simchat Torah*, published in 5637/1877). The service included the liturgy for the three *haqafot* (13f, 16f, 25f) as well as the longest *kaddish* in the world (35-40).

Arbith prayers followed the unique *Mincha,* and following them was another unique Cochin observance, which was especially intriguing. The Torah scrolls were placed on chairs and benches, and everyone, men, women, and children sang *shir'ot* in the synagogue hall, the congregation dismantled the temporary ark. It was demolished ritually and methodically: the Banarsi silks were carefully removed, followed by the silver pillars. Finally the wooden planks were disassembled. Throughout there were *shir'ot*, and at the end the young people started singing and dancing an Israeli folk dance, the *hora*. After they were finished with dismantling the ark, the Israeli national anthem, *Hatiqvah* (The Hope), was sung.

Once again the Jew Town folks walked from their synagogue to the tiny street, this time with measured steps and restrained demeanor. As they walked past the blazing tree of light, the slow steps of Sattu Koder set the pace. The entire community escorted the eldest member to the door of his house, sneaking longing glances back to the metal-and-fire tree. The restraint of this final ritual act of the fall cycle was a striking counterpoint to the animated ark dismantling and *hora* dancing. Everyone sang the Indian national anthem, a counterbalance to *Hatiqvah*. Just before entering the doorway, Sattu proclaimed with a wave, "God bless everyone," and everyone replied in one voice, *"L'shanah haba b'Yerushalaym"* ("Next year in Jerusalem!"). Someone thought to adapt the Hebrew adage to better fit their circumstances and shouted out, *"L'shanah haba b'Cochin"* ("Next year in Cochin!"), a rallying cry that echoed along Synagogue Lane until everyone had retired into their homes, exhausted from a full month of festivals.

The three aspects of the Cochin *minhagim* for Simchat Torah which are the creative responses to their Hindu environment in Kerala are the displaying of their Torah scrolls on a temporary ark, the addition of afternoon *haqafot* outside of the synagogue building, and the ritual dismantling of the ark. For this, specific Hinduized symbols of royalty and nobility have been appropriated.

Hindu practice is always defined by a particular community of Hindus, determined by caste and geography, as well as other factors. There is no one normative version of Hinduism, but rather a dazzling array of local traditions. As we have seen, the symbols of royalty and nobility are generally promoted by the dominant caste of the region, which in Kerala is the Nayar caste, and in Cochin the Perumpaddapu family in particular.

Like most of the royal families, the Perumpaddapus are devotees of Lord Krsna, the erotic warrior-prince God of the Vaisnava pantheon. The maharaja's temple, which abuts the Cochin Synagogue, is known as the Pazhayannur Sri Krsna Temple, and it is not surprising that the Indian nobility opted to worship a God who sprang from their own community of rulers and warriors. What enabled the Jews to adapt the symbols of a royal Hindu God were their own metaphors of God's kingship (*malchut*), the dominant liturgical theme for the High Holy Days. What was required was an exaggeration of ritual themes inherent in Judaism, not the adoption of alien symbols.

Each and every Hindu temple has its own deity and a periodic, usually annual, festival for that deity. During the festival the deity's image is generally displayed on a wooden cart. Often these carts are enormous, such as the one in the famous cart festival at the Sri Jagannath Temple in Puri, Orissa. More than a million Hindus participate in Sri Jagannath's festival, pulling the 300-foot cart down Puri's main road. At the conclusion of such temple festivals, the deity's image is ceremoniously disposed of, often by immersing it into a river or the ocean.

The three elements characteristic of Hindu temple festivals, display, procession, and disposal, are also characteristic of Simchat Torah in Cochin. Like a Hindu deity the Torah scrolls are removed from their usual holy abode, the Jewish *aron hakodesh*, paralleling the Hindu *sanctum sanctorum*, and displayed on a temporary structure, the Jewish temporary ark, paralleling the Hindu cart. Like the deity they are carried through a public area, in this case the synagogue courtyard. As the deity's image is disposed of at the end of the festival, so the temporary ark—not of course the Torah scrolls—is demolished ritually. It is precisely these three aspects of the Cochin *minhagim* which are so unique and which serve as the means by which Hindu royalty symbols and rituals are adapted and Judaized.

The ingenuity of these adaptations is an instance of the Jewish genius for cultural adaptation. How to participate in the Gentile world while maintaining fidelity to Jewish observance has been the challenge faced by Jews in all four corners of the Diaspora. In India, a culture not merely tolerant of religious diversity but affectionately supportive of it, Jews have adapted to Hinduism while adhering to normative Judaism's standards. Theirs has been a well-balanced, ritually established identity. Traditional Jewish metaphors and symbols of nobility and royalty have been judiciously merged with borrowings from Hindu practice in order to connect Jews with one of India's poles of power and thereby to integrate the Jews into Kerala's predominantly Hindu social order.

Concluding Remarks

The Cochin Jews provide a particularly fine example of how a small religio-ethnic community can locate itself within a larger society. By a periodic ritual enactment of the symbols representing the poles of power in the caste hierarchy of Kerala, a secure place in that hierarchy is achieved. In some instances strands from within the guest community's traditions that are congruent with, or parallel to, the symbols of the host's culture are adapted, while in other cases the host's symbols are borrowed directly. By so doing the guest community retains its unique identity, while at the same time finding a place within the larger host society.

Sources cited

"Asceticism". 1910. *The Encyclopaedia Britannica.* 11th ed., vol. II, 717-720. Cambridge and New York: Cambridge University Press.

Berman, Rabbi Jacob. 1978 & 1982. *Popular Halacha*: A Guide to *Jewish Living* . 2 vols. Jerusalem: World Zionist Organization.

"Caste". 1987. *The Encyclopaedia of Asian History: A Selection of Sample Articles.* Ed. Ainslee Embree. New York: Charles Scribner's Sons.

Chill, Rabbi Abraham. 1979. *The Minhagim: The Customs and Ceremonies of Judaism, Their Origins and Rationale.* New York: Sepher-Hermon Press.

Cohen, Rabbi Jacob. 1970. *The Royal Table: An Outline of the Dietary Laws of Isreal.* Jerusalem and New York: Feldheim.

Cohen, Yaakob Daniel, ed. 5637/1877. *Seder Mincha Simchat Torah.* Cochin: Y.D. Cohen.

Dobrinsky, Herbert C. 1986. *A Treasury of Sephardic Laws and Customs: The Ritual Practices of Syrian, Moroccan, Judeo-Spanish and Spanish and Portuguese Jews of North America.* Hoboken, NJ: Ktav Publishing House, and New York: Yeshiva University Press.

Dumont, Louis. 1980. *Homo Hierarchicus: The Caste System and Its Implications.* Chicago and London: University of Chicago Press.

Dutt, Manmatha Nath. 1977. *The Dharma Shastra, or The Hindu Law Codes.* Varanasi: Chaukhamba Amarbharati Prakashan, Chaukhamba Amarbharati Studies, vol. V.

'Edeni, Eliahu. 1688. *Seder Azharot I'Rabbi Eliahu ha Edeni biMinhag Kogin.* Amsterdam: Proops.

Edgerton, Franklin. 1977. *Buddhist Hybrid Sanskrit Dictionary.* Delhi: Motilal Banarsidass.

Fischel, Walter J. 1973. *Unknown Jews in Unknown Lands: The Travels of Rabbi David D'Beth Hillel* (1824-1832). New York: Ktav.

————. 1981. "The Present State of Research on the History of the Jews in India from the 16th Century On," *Jewish Tradition in the Diaspora: Studies in Memory of Walter J. Fischel,* 23-33. Ed. Misheal Maswari Caspi. Berkeley, CA: Judah L. Magnes Museum.

————. 1982. "The Jews in Mediaeval Iran from the 16th to the 17th Centuries: Political, Economic, and Communal Aspects," *Irano-Judaica: Studies Relating to Jewish Contacts with Persian Culture Throughout the Ages,* 265-291. Ed. Saul Shaked. Jerusalem: Ben Zvi Institute.

Fredman, Ruth Gerber. 1981. *The Passover Seder.* New York:

New American Library.

Ganzfried, Rabbi Solomon. 1961. *Kitzur Shulchan 'Arukh: Code of Jewish Law*. Trans. Hyman E. Goldin. New York: Hebrew Publishing Co.

Hall, T.C. 1958. "Asceticism (Introduction)," *Encyclopaedia of Religion and Ethics*, vol. II, 63-69. Ed. James Hastings, New York: Charies Scribner's Sons.

Hallegua, I. S. 1988. *The Paradesi Synagogue of Cochin and Its Dying Community of Jews*. Cochin: photocopied ms. for private circulation by author.

Hallegua, S.H. 1986. "Simchat Torah in Cochin," *Kol Bina* 6/1:6.

Jacobs, Louis. 1987. "Passover", *The Encyclopaedia of Religion,* vol. II, 204-206. Ed. Mircea Eliade. New York: Macmillans.

Johnson, Barbara C. 1985. "'Our Community' in Two Worlds: The Cochin Paradesi Jews in India and Isreal." Ph.D. dissertation, University of Massachusetts.

—————. 1986. "The Emperor's Welcome: Reconsiderations of an Origin Theme in Cochin Jewish Folklore," *Jews in India,* 161-176. Ed. Thomas A. Timberg. New Delhi: Vikas.

Kaelber, Walter O. 1987. "Asceticism", *The Encyclopaedia of Religion,* vol. 1, 441-445. Ed. Mircea Eliade. New York: Macmilans.

Katz, Nathan, and Goldberg, Ellen S. 1988. "The Last Jews in India and Burma," *Jerusalem Letter* 101:1-8.

—————. 1989. "Asceticism and Caste in the Passover Observances of the Cochin Jews," *Journal of the American Academy of Religion* 57/1:52-83.

—————. 1993. *The Last Jews of Cochin: Jewish Identity in Hindu India*. Columbia, SC : University of South Carolina Press.

—————. 1988/1993. "Jewish Apartheid and a Jewish Gandhi," *Jewish Social Studies* 50, 4: 147-176

Machazor Shingli ["Shingli Beth"]. 1769. Amsterdam: Proops.

Machazor L'Yomim Noraim. n.d. Amsterdam: Proops.

Maimonides. 1988. *Rambam Mishneh Torah Hilchot Chametz U'Matzah*. Trans. Rabbi Eliyahu Touger. New York and

Jerusalem: Moznaim Publishing Co.

Mandelbaum, David G. 1939. "The Jewish Way of Life in Cochin," *Jewish Social Studies* 1/4:423-460.

——————. 1981. "A Case History of Judaism: The Jews of Cochin in India and in Isreal," *Jewish Tradition in the Diaspora: Studies in Memory of Walter J. Fischel,* 211-230. Ed. Maswari Caspi. Berkeley: Judah L. Magnes Museum.

Marriott, McKim. 1959. "Interactional and Attributional Theories of Caste Ranking," *Man in India* 39/2:92-107.

Neusner, Jacob. 1973. *The Idea of Purity in Ancient Judaism.* Leiden: E.J. Brill.

Pool, David de Sola, ed. & tr. 1986 [1941]. *Seder HaTefilot: Book of Prayers According to the Custom of the Spanish and Portuguese Jews.* 2nd ed. New York: Union of Sephardic Congregations.

Rader, Rosemary. 1987. "Fasting," *The Encyclopaedia of Religion*, vol. 5, 286-290. Ed. Mircea Eliade. New York: Macmillans.

Reinman, Shlomo. 1984. "Masa'oth Shlomo b'Kogin," *Mikotsin l'Eretz Yisroel*, 31-39. Ed. Shalva Weil. Jerusalem: Kumu Brinah.

Salem, Avraham Baruch. 1929. *Eternal Light or Jewtown Synagogue.* (Ernakulam: S.D. Printing Works.)

Saphir, Yaacov. 1984. "HaYehudim b'Kogin," *MiKotsin l'Eretz Yisroel*, 21-30. Ed. Shalva Weil. Jerusalem: Kumu Brinah.

Schneerson, Rabbi Menachem M. 1985. *Haggadah for Pesach, with an Anthology of Reasons and Customs.* Trans. Jacob Immanuel Shochet. Brooklyn: Qehot.

Simon, A.I. 1947. " The Songs of the Jews of Cochin and their Historical Significance," *Bulletin of the Rama Varma Research Institute* 13.

Smith, Jonathan Z. 1982. *Imagining Religion from Babylon to Jonestown.* Chicago and London: University of Chicago Press.

——————. 1987. *To Take Place: Toward Theory in Ritual.* Chicago and London: University of Chicago Press.

Timberg, Thomas A., ed. 1986. *Jews in India.* New Delhi: Vikas; New York: Advent.

Turner, Victor W. 1977. *The Ritual Process: Structure and Anti-Structure*. Ithaca: Cornell University Press.

Weinberg, Werner. 1976. *How Do You Spell Chanukah? A General-Purpose Romanization of Hebrew for Speakers of English*. Cincinnati: Hebrew Union College.

Whitney, William Dwight. 1945. *The Roots, Verb-Forms and Primary Derivatives of the Sanskrit Language*. New Haven: American Oriental Society, American Oriental Series vol. 30 [1885].

Zalman, Rabbi Schneur, ed. 1985. *Shulchan 'Arukh Orech Chayyim*. 4 vols. Brooklyn: Qehot.

Interviews and conversations with the Jew Town folks—Jacob E. Cohen, Sarah Cohen, Gamliel Salem, Reema Salem, Sattu S. Koder, Isaac Ashkenazy, I.S. Hallegua, Elias Koder, Raymond Salem, Sammy Hallegua, Queenie Hallegua, Fiona Hallegua, Yosef Hallegua, Jackie Cohen—and their friends, the late D.B. "Bapusait" Khona and P.M. Jussay.

2

"For Any Good Occasion We Call Them": Community Parties and Cultural Continuity among the Cochin Paradesi Jews of Israel[1]

Barbara C. Johnson

Maintaining group identity in the process of transition from one cultural world to another is a challenge which has faced Jews throughout their long history of migration from country to country, from continent to continent. This article examines the centrality of a particular ritual event—the community party or *peshta*—in preserving community identity among one group of new Israelis from Kerala State in South India, those associated originally with the Paradesi Synagogue in Jew Town, Cochin.

Back in Jew Town today, visitors to the exquisite Paradesi Synagogue join with the remaining handful of fewer than 30 Jews, along with their Hindu, Muslim and Christian neighbors, in bemoaning the immanent demise of this 400-year-old Jewish congregation. In contrast, little notice is taken of the community's new branch in Israel, where a lively ritual and social life is maintained for approximately 200 members of the group who now call themselves "Cochinites". As pointed out recently by Ruby Daniel, one of the oldest members of this new Paradesi community

[1] Fieldwork research on community parties in 1981 and 1982 was carried out under grants from the Social Science Research Council, the Fulbright-Hays Doctoral Dissertation Abroad Program, the Danforth Foundation, and the Memorial Foundation for Jewish Culture. I am particularly grateful to Rachel Roby, Sassoon Roby and the late Balfour Salem for their recent explanations of several elements in the 1988 *erev brit* ritual. This article is dedicated to the memory of Balfour Salem, Raymond Salem, Daniel and Rachel Hallegua, who were participants in that event.

in Israel, "Some people write that [our] Cochin community of Jews is dying. They don't realize that a root from that tree is shooting up in Israel and starting to blossom" (Daniel and Johnson 1995).

Since 1981 I have been working to document this process of transplanting and blossoming, showing elements of continuity amidst the inevitable and sometimes overwhelming changes which face any group making such a move from one cultural world to another (Johnson 1985). Examining ritual assertions of cultural identity, I first analyzed the centrality of Passover preparations and celebrations in Cochin as markers of Jewish separateness from their non-Jewish neighbors. Whereas these practices fit well with the dominant Hindu emphasis on purity and pollution in defining community boundaries, they do not play the same role in Israel. Rather than setting them apart, Passover in Israel becomes an occasion for Cochinite integration into the Jewish mainstream.

At first glance, Paradesi life-cycle rituals in Israel also appeared to be occasions for cultural assimilation, especially those weddings, *b'nai mitzvah* and circumcisions which are held in a rented *ulam* or public hall to the accompaniment of Israeli food and popular music. But closer acquaintance with the community reveals the importance of home-based evening celebrations which precede and parallel such public events. My observation since 1981 is that the community party or *peshta* has increased in centrality as the expanding community celebrates more and more life-cycle rituals. Far from being replaced by more public rituals, the home-based *peshta* is evolving as a treasured event filled with Kerala style and content, a primary mechanism of cultural continuity for the community or *kambooLam*.

In extending personal invitations to a party, it is essential to include the entire *kambooLam*. "*NamoDe kambooLam*" ("our community" in colloquial Jewish Malayalam) is seen by its core members in Israel as a direct continuation of the community they left behind in India. In Jewish Malayalam usage, the phrase literally means "our street", referring to Synagogue Lane in Jew Town where almost all the Paradesi Jews lived.[2] By extension it refers to all the Jews who lived on that street and worshipped at the Paradesi Synagogue, along with others who have been incorporated into the group.

In Israel today the Paradesi community of about 200 people includes a number of "Bombay Cochinites" whose Paradesi ancestors left Kerala for Bombay several generations ago, and a growing number of non-Indians who have entered the group by marriage. New members are socialized in community customs and values partly by attending parties. Some Cochinites even define membership in their Israeli community by who is invited to and who regularly attends the *peshtas*. "For every good occasion we call them" is one way of affirming that possibly marginal community members really do belong. The core population who once lived in Jew Town are members by definition, whether or not they attend the *peshtas*, but when I asked about the status of some others I was told "Yes, [certain people are community members] because they come to our parties," or "No, I can't count *them* because they are never at parties."

Within the cultural context of South India, the Cochin branch of the *kambooLam* has always been highly visible. Encountering them in Jew Town, outsiders labelled them "Paradesis" (foreigners) or "White Jews" because certain prominent members of their group retain the fair complexions of Middle Eastern or Spanish ancestors who immigrated to Cochin as long ago as the early sixteenth century. Some of the Paradesis originally came to India as merchants and some sought refuge from persecution. Arriving in Cochin they joined a much more ancient group of Kerala Jews, whose ancestors probably came to this Malabar coast of southwest India as far back as 2000 years ago, and who had seven thriving congregations with well-established synagogues in the Cochin area. After the arrival of the so-called "Whites," some people

---

[2]In standard Malayalam "kambooLam" means market. See Johnson (1985, 1994) for a discussion of *community* rather than caste or ethnicity as the key unit for analyzing Paradesi group identity.

began calling the original Malabari Jews "Black," a label which many of them resent. In fact not all of the "White Jews" are fair-skinned, nor are all of the so-called "Black Jews" of Kerala dark-skinned; the labels refer to community membership rather than strictly to complexion.

In 1568 the Paradesis built their own synagogue at the end of the main street of Jew Town, on land given to them by the Hindu maharaja next to his palace. A significant number of the newcomers must have been women as well as men, for they did not intermarry with most of the original Kerala or Malabari Jews. But these "foreigners" soon became thoroughly Indian as a community, adopting the Malayalam language, the Kerala food and dress, and certain uniquely South Indian Jewish traditions. In fact some Paradesis identified so strongly with their adopted home that they claimed to be the authentic descendants of the original Jewish immigrants to the ancient port of nearby Cranganore—a claim that was vigorously rejected by the larger and older community of Kerala Jews (Johnson 1975, 1985).

Beginning in the early 1950s, almost all of the original Kerala or Malabari Jews migrated to Israel. Now called "Cochinim" in Israeli Hebrew, they are set off today as an Israeli *edah* or ethnic group of more than 4000 people, whose identity centers in five agricultural *moshavim* and a number of urban neighborhoods.[3] Their performances of cultural identity have been documented by folklorist Marcia Walerstein (1987), who has also written of their successful integration into the Israeli economy after an initially difficult period of adjustment. (See also Abraham 1989, Kushner 1973, Moskowitz 1986, Shokeid 1971.)

Though some Paradesis maintain friendly relations with particular Cochini families, they do not identify themselves and are not seen by others as part of this Cochini *edah*. Very few Paradesis joined the Malabaris in their mass *aliyah* of the 1950s. The Paradesi

---

[3] Their population increased from approximately 2500 in the early 1950s, apparently due to a fairly high birth rate, along with the incorporation of Cochin Jews who had lived in Bombay and marriage with non-Cochinim.

migration to Israel has been a gradual process, beginning in the early 1970s, as has the subsequent reconstitution of their community in Israel.

In contrast to the Cochinim, the Paradesis ("Cochinites") in Israel have gone almost unnoticed by outsiders. They number only about 200 people and have no geographical center comparable to the Cochini *moshavim*. Even in the small town of Binyamina where there are several Paradesi households, they are outnumbered in the synagogue. A few Cochinite men take the lead in conducting services and introduce some of their traditional tunes, but they frequently voice the complaint that the synagogue is not "ours". As a group, the Cochinites experience little external boundary reinforcement from outsiders. With many of their fair-skinned members not even identifiable as Indian by other Israelis, their internal boundary-maintenance mechanisms must remain strong in order to preserve a sense of community identity.

The following ethnographic descriptions show some of the ways in which community parties reinforce this sense of identity. Three types will be described—*peshtas* for a *chanukat habayit* or housewarming, for the religious holiday of Simchat Torah, and for *erev brit*, the evening before a circumcision.

Cochinite Parties: A Descriptive Overview

Paradesi parties in Israel must be seen within the context of a constant pattern of visiting and hospitality within the community. On any given weekend, it is usual to find several Cochinite families and individuals gathered in one place, resulting in a large group dinner for Friday night or Saturday noon. Or there might be a small party somewhere in the community, celebrating a birthday or the arrival of visitor. Even if such a gathering involves 25 to 30 guests, it would not be called a *peshta*. A *peshta* involves extensive advance preparation and an open invitation to everyone in the community; all who can make it are expected to attend. It is called for some specific celebration, whether a family event or a Jewish holiday. And it must include a *minyan* of ten men, for prayers before and after the meal.

Each *peshta* combines religious ritual with a large Kerala-style meal and plenty of time for socializing. In each party, continuities with Jew Town life are apparent—in the framed picture of the Paradesi Synagogue found on the wall of almost every Cochinite apartment, in the lively laughter and exchange of community news in a mixture of Malayalam, English and Hebrew, and of course in the familiar aromas and spicy flavors of South Indian food.

Food is often acknowledged as a quintessential symbol of ethnic identity, and recent research has focused on the process of making and consuming it as well as on the food itself (Brown and Mussell 1985, Kalcik 1985). Food for a *peshta* evokes a vivid sensory continuity with India. Not surprisingly, it is prepared elaborately and in vast quantities. There must always be enough food—that is, much more than enough to serve everyone. Back in Cochin the food and other arrangements for a party would have been made with the help of non-Jewish servants, but in Israel much of the preparatory work falls on older Cochinite women who do not work outside of their homes and on younger women in the community who take a few days leave from work. Indian cooking takes time, and with many women in the community employed in full-time jobs, not every family manages to eat rice and curry on a daily basis. All the more reason to look forward to a party!

Two different types of food are served in two distinct parts of any *peshta*: pre-dinner snacks and a main meal based on rice. On ordinary days the two types of eating are separated in time, but festive meals must begin with appetizers.

Though many different snacks are served at the beginning of a *peshta*, the essential one is the traditional Cochin Jewish *pastel*, a pastry stuffed with ground meat and served on Shabbat and holidays with a fenugreek-based sauce called *hilba*. A common item in various Sephardic and Middle Eastern cuisines, the *pastel* is marked as a peculiarly Jewish food in Cochin; but over the generations it has taken on its own Indian identity, so that it is now marked as an Indian food by Cochinites in Israel.[4]   Different women in the community have their own ways of making *pastels*—varying the stuffing mix and opting to either bake or fry the pastry—and insiders are likely to compliment each cook for her particular style. But the point is that *pastels* must be served to guests, in Cochin or in Israel, for any festive occasion.

As is customary in South India, the meal itself is based on large amounts of rice, cooked for special occasions with spices as a *pillau*. Meat and fish are also essential for festive meals. A typical party menu features at least one fish or fish ball curry, several different chicken curries and sometimes beef or vegetable curries too. Some of the recipes are particular to Indian Jewish cooking, like the Baghdadi-style *kubha* (dumpling) curry borrowed from the Calcutta and Bombay Jews; and of course all of them are subject to the universally Jewish restrictions of *kashrut*. Non-Indian food is incorporated only in a few optional snacks and in Israeli vegetable salads.

In Cochin the festive meal would have been served in formal style, the tables arranged in the shape of the Hebrew letter *bet*, with the honored persons seated at the head in the central section.[5] In a crowded two-bedroom Israeli apartment, serving and eating must of necessity be buffet-style. Plastic plates with plastic utensils also contribute to a less formal atmosphere.

In addition to the cultural continuities embodied in food, particular religious rituals have been incorporated into *peshtas* in Israel, providing further continuity with Jew Town life. One important element of Cochin Jewish culture is the presence of many unique prayers and religious melodies. Without a synagogue of their own in Israel, Cochinites show creative flexibility in shifting certain of these rituals into the framework of their community parties.

Prayers and songs are led by the older Paradesi men, with

---

[4]In Cochin a *pastel* is a pastry filled with ground meat and perhaps potatoes or eggs, whereas a similar cheese-filled pastry is called a *bureka*.

[5]Rachel Roby, 4/12/92.

women and younger men joining in at important moments. But it would be artificial to label the men's role as religious and the women's as secular. In a very real sense this continuity of religious ritual is made possible by the strenuous labor of the older Cochinite women who spend so many hours and days preparing a *peshta*. Echoing Susan Sered (1988:137), it could be said that in their cooking and many other arrangements for a party these women are engaged in a very spiritual task: strengthening "the networks of relationship that make sacred human existence."

Housewarming Parties

Each of the first two community parties which I attended in 1981 was a *chanukat habayit*, the dedication of a home or a housewarming. Both were held in apartments which were not actually new, and both incorporated additional reasons for the community to come together. Leslie and Glenys Salem, a young married couple, had lived in their Haifa apartment for over a year, and were combining a *chanukat habayit* with a celebration of their daughter's first birthday and a farewell to Leslie's mother, who was about to return to Cochin after a long visit. Later that year in Binyamina, Mrs. Essie Ashkenazy and her two adult daughters hosted a *chanukat habayit* on completing major renovations to their apartment. They were also celebrating the arrival of Eric, their son and brother, who had recently come to Israel.

Arriving four days before the Binyamina party, I found the hostess Essie in the kitchen with her friend, Koko Roby, who had come from Petah Tikvah to help. They had already made about 130 *pastels*. The next morning they prepared fish ball curry and their non-dairy version of the Indian dessert *paayasam* for the party, in addition to doing the usual weekly cooking for Shabbat. Early Sunday morning they were back in the kitchen again. Joined by two more out-of-town visitors and Essie's daughters, who had taken time off from work, they produced three different kinds of chicken curry, a beef curry, several salads, and some Western-style dinner rolls. On the day of the party, huge pots of rice *pillau* were put on to cook, as the young people worked on arranging the apartment. Guests continued arriving throughout the afternoon by bus and car at the different local Cochinite homes where they would later spend the night.

The format of each *chanukat habayit* was the same. By early evening the party had officially begun, with an extended round of greetings. All the furniture in the small apartment had been pushed to the wall. Some people were sitting on chairs on the sides, but more were milling about, going from one person to the next, greeting each other with warm handshakes and kisses, exchanging inquiries, small items of news, and expressions of delight. Popular Israeli and American music was blaring loudly on the stereo set, overseen by some of the young people who had brought record albums.

When almost everyone had gathered, the music was turned off and the oldest man present began the group recitation of *Arbith*, the daily evening prayer service (which in Cochin would have been recited in the synagogue). All the older man participated, along with some of the older women and younger men; some prayed from memory and some from Hebrew prayer books which they had brought with them. The atmosphere was relaxed; children ran in and out, women continued to bustle about in the kitchen area, and a few more guests arrived. Occasionally someone would let out a loud but ineffective "Shhhh!" to try to restore a bit more order.

The next stage of the party found people helping themselves to drinks and appetizers, which had been set out on tables near the kitchen area. Hard liquor, beer, liqueurs and soft drinks were in liberal supply along with the *pastels* and other snacks. The loud music resumed, and animated conversation continued everywhere. Some people began to dance in the crowded living room, while others talked around the edges. Some of the dances were done by couples and other were group-oriented circle dances. People of all ages participated—children, teenagers, single persons and married couples—and eventually it was announced that games would begin. At both house warming parties there was a lively game of "pass the parcel" involving humorous "forfeits"; many of

the women participated and most of the men and children watched
with great amusement.

Finally it was time for the meal, which was served buffet-
style on tables near the kitchen. People ate standing or sitting in
every available space. The cooks kept refilling the serving dishes,
and seemed pleased with the many compliments. At the Binyamina
party the hostess and main cook told me several times: "Thank God
it is all turning out well!"

When the eating was over, a traditional Hebrew *birkat
hamazon* (blessing after the meal) was recited by a few of the men.
Then all attention was directed to the ritual climax of the *peshta*: the
extremely enthusiastic chanting of a set of blessings on the family
whose house was being dedicated. Those who were to be blessed
were seated on chairs, while others stood around them, some
placing hands on their heads. At the Haifa party, Seema Salem
placed one hand on the head of her son and one on the head of her
daughter-in-law; while others placed their hands on Seema's
head, and also on the young couple. In Binyamina the hands of
blessing were placed on members of the Ashkenazy family. At this
point the chant-like singing rose in volume and in focus, ending
with the Cochin version of Psalm 111 "Halleluyah odeh", and the
final Hebrew words:

> "All the blessings generally are to Israel and the family of the
> host and hostess. May the Lord preserve and keep you all alive
> with good health, peace, perfect healings and redemptions to all
> the relations, and say Amen."

Many participants punctuated their singing with vigorous and
rhythmic hand-clapping, and a few older women ended with a burst
of ululation. This same blessing had marked the conclusion of a *bar
mitzvah* dinner I attended in Cochin in 1977, and I was to see it
enacted at many other Cochin events.

The blessing marked the formal ending of the *peshta*—the
point at which a number of participants seemed to sense that the
event was over and began to say goodbye. At the Haifa party, they

circulated around the apartment, taking leave of each other with lengthy and sometimes emotional farewells. Though many were staying in other Cochinite homes in Haifa, they would have to leave early in the morning for work. (At the Binyamina party, the next day was Election Day, a secular holiday, so many would be staying on for card-playing and a trip to the beach). They were already talking about plans for the next community party, as well as for getting together in smaller groups in the meantime. In the kitchen area, clean-up activities were just beginning and would continue into the night, carried out and supervised by the same women who had done the cooking. Meanwhile, out-of-town guests scattered to the various Cochinite apartments in town, where the merry-making continued. All spare sofas were occupied, and quilts and blankets were spread on the floor. Conversation went on even after the lights were out, and stories would be exchanged later about witty remarks and pranks that continued in the separate apartments.

A Simchat Torah Party

In Cochin the festival of Simchat Torah, concluding the period of the High Holy Days, was the ritual and social high point of the Jewish year. Each synagogue was decorated like a bride, hung with fragrant flower garlands and brilliantly colored silk. The entire community gathered in festival finery to celebrate the reading of the final Torah portion for the year and of the first portion for the new year.

As in all Jewish communities, the Torah scrolls were carried with songs and dancing in seven *haqafot* (circular processions) inside the synagogue, on the eve and morning of the holiday. In addition, all eight congregations of Cochin Jews had a unique tradition which they trace back to their Cranganore ancestors. They always added an extra celebration on the afternoon of Simchat Torah for the *Mincha* service. Carrying the Torah scrolls in their heavy silver cases outside the synagogue, they would circumambulate the building three times, singing a special set of songs said to have been composed in Cranganore and sung to what they call "Shingli tunes". These songs are found in a small printed book used only for this occasion.[6]

Simchat Torah in Cochin was a day for drinking and boisterous merrymaking, in which the Jewish social structure was temporarily turned around, as on Purim or the Hindu festival of Holi. On the street, young people gleefully threw water and raw eggs at each other and at their elders. This was the only holiday on which women were welcome inside the main part of the synagogue, where they joined the men in the processions and singing. Liquor flowed freely in the synagogue compound during the afternoon *haqafot*. As I was told over and over, you cannot know what "our community" is unless you have been in Cochin for Simchat Torah.

How can the celebration of this festival be transferred effectively to Israel, where the Paradesi Cochinites have no synagogue of their own in which to celebrate? To hear them talk about it in advance, there simply is no comparison—but anyway, they congregate in Binyamina for synagogue services and a party. I needed no urging to attend this event.[7]

The 1981 Simchat Torah celebration in Binyamina, like any community party, began with the arrival of guests from all parts of Israel. This *peshta* was to be a potluck meal, so many of the arriving Cochinites brought dishes and vessels of food, which they dropped off at the apartment where the meal would be held. But on this

[6]This Simchat Torah *Mincha* book was the first Hebrew printed book in Cochin, hand-set in Hebrew type at the Ashkenazy family press in 1877. Shingli is the Cochin Jewish name for the ancient city of Cranganore, their first home in India. See Johnson 1975:106-115 for a discussion of Shingli tunes and 147-154 for a comparison of this Jewish ritual with religious customs of their Hindu, Muslim and Christian neighbors.

[7]In contrast, Malabari Cochinim from all over Israel congregate for Simchat Torah at Moshav Nevatim, where they have built a synagogue in the Kerala pattern, incorporating a wooden Ark and a Torah scroll with a silver case and gold crown which were brought from one of the Kerala synagogues. See Walerstein 1987 for a detailed description of this celebration, and for an analysis of the centrality of Simchat Torah as a symbol of Cochini identity in Israel.

occasion the festivities actually began at the small Chaim Ohel Yaakov Synagogue, where the Binyamina Cochinites regularly worship along with a majority of Iraqis, Georgians and Jews from other *edot*. On Simchat Torah (in contrast to an ordinary Shabbat) the approximately 70 Cochinites outnumbered other worshippers and set the tone for the evening. Cochin tunes dominated, though Iraqi tunes were also used. Wine was available on a side table, as the men took turns carrying the Torah scrolls in joyous *haqafot* inside the synagogue. Most were dancing and jumping up and down while they sang and paraded. In deference to non-Cochinite custom, the women had to stay in their own section rather than join the processions as they used to do in Cochin; but they too sang at full volume, and the children ran about excitedly or rode on the men's shoulders, waving small paper flags. Non-Cochinites joined in, but there was no doubt that the South Indian *minhag* prevailed. I wrote in my notes afterward:

> Many people asked me . . . if I had been in Cochin for Simchat Torah, and they told me how beautiful it is there—the special oil lamp outside, the silk cloths hanging, the smell of jasmine flowers, the colors. . . . This is nothing in comparison, they said over and over. But that night it didn't feel like a complaint. Everyone was so high, it was part of the elation to talk about Cochin, to somehow include Cochin in the event. But the event was very much in the present (10/19/81).

After services small Cochinite groups first congregated in several different apartments for drinks, *pastels* and other snacks, before meeting together about 70-strong at Sammy and Simmy Koder's apartment. The Koders host a Simchat Torah party each year to celebrate Simmy's birthday as well as the holiday on which it occurs. The structure of this party was looser than that of a *chanukat habayit*. High-spirited drinking continued full force, with many humorous toasts, and the potluck meal was served with rice, curries, salads and Indian snacks which had been prepared in many different kitchens.

In the course of the evening various old books appeared at a table where a number of men were seated. Among them were the small books of Shingli songs associated with the special afternoon *haqafot* outside the synagogue in Cochin. A core group of men sitting at the table sang through the whole book, while other men and a number of women joined in with vigor on particular tunes. I understand that nowadays the three unique afternoon Cochin *haqafot* are conducted at the synagogue in Binyamina, so these special songs have been restored to their appropriate time of day and thus are no longer sung at the party the evening before. But the point is that the Shingli songs are not lost. In 1981 they were at the heart of the *peshta*.

When the meal was over and the singing ended, the *birkat hamazon* was recited. On this occasion there was no "Halleluyah odeh" blessing, but I later learned that this most popular song must have been sung already without my realizing it, as it originates in the special *Mincha* liturgy for Simchat Torah.[8] Still, there was a musical climax to this party, as with every *peshta* I have attended. It consisted of everyone singing the Hebrew song "Tzur mishelo" to a popular Cochin tune which has set variations for different ritual occasions. The singing rose to a pitch of loudness and fervor which surpassed even the customary "Halleluyah" blessing— perhaps because of the quantity of liquor which had been consumed. "We spent a remarkably long time singing 'Tzur mishelo'," I wrote in my notes: "By this time almost all were standing, Nappy taking the lead along with Morris, and every time it seemed the song was about to end, one of them would prolong the line 'sabanu, sabanu, sabanu' ['we have eaten our fill'] over and over, then start in again with vigor on 'Tzur mishelo.'"

It took a long time for people to settle down in different apartments that night, as the laughter and joking continued, but

---

[8]"Halleluyah odeh" is sung at the most joyous moment when the Torah scroll is removed from the Ark, and also when it is returned to the Ark at the conclusion of the *haqafot*. See the book of Cochin Jewish songs and rituals published in Ashdod, Israel: *Areshet Sefatenu* (1979), pp. 203-304. My thanks to Ruby Daniel and Sassoon Roby for pointing out these connections.

finally the sleeping arrangements were sorted out. The next morning's service at the synagogue seemed considerably more subdued, and the drinking in the afternoon was also more contained. The young people did manage to run off with the egg supply from several kitchens and staged a rowdy egg fight in the parking lot, to the wonder and amusement of some non-Cochinite neighbors. My attempt to resume the anthropologist's role (despite a severe hangover) and photograph this part of the festivities was foiled when my attention was called to a young Cochinite named Ezzie, up in the second storey window, who was having a dishpan of cold water poured over his head. An egg was smashed on my head at this very moment, and it seemed more appropriate to wipe the yolk off my camera case, put the equipment aside and join in the chase.

A Brit Mila Party

In January 1988, a direct descendant of the nineteenth century Paradesi elder, Eliya Roby, was born in Israel. This baby, who was given the Israeli name Shaked, is a descendant in the twelfth generation of the Jewish merchant Ezekiel Rahabi, who came from Aleppo to Cochin in 1646, and the first member of this particular branch of the Roby family to be born in the new land of Israel. His mother Sandra Roby Tuwig immigrated to Israel with her family as a young girl in the early 1970s. Shaked's birth was of course celebrated with a traditional Jewish circumcision ritual, and also—like all "good occasions"—with a community party the night before.

Just hours after the birth of her grandson, Rachel (Rachu) Roby was on the phone, spreading the good news. "*Kol ha kambooLam* we must call," Rachu explained to me, her mother-in-law Koko echoing the words "*kol ha kambooLam*" "the entire community". In a mixture of Malayalam, Hebrew and English (characteristic of much Cochinite conversation), she gave the details to members of the community throughout Israel and even in Cochin:

Black curly hair, round face. Quite big, *nalla* (beautifully) chubby. *Oru mani* (one o'clock), I tried to call you. You knew already? Monday *brit* (circumcision), *b'ezrat Hashem* (with God's help). *Todah, todah* (thank you, thank you). *Mila* (circumcision) Monday, Monday *b'ezrat Hashem. Erev* (night before) *brit* we will make the *Havdaliyah*, so you must come. *Brit* Tel Aviv. Havdallah *rathri* (night) Sunday night.

According to Jewish law, the *brit mila* or circumcision ritual would take place eight days after the birth. The circumcision ritual itself—and an especially elaborate public celebration for the family's first grandchild—was to be held the following Monday afternoon in a rented hall in Tel Aviv. About 300 invited guests, perhaps half of them from outside the community, would be notified of the time and place by a formal engraved invitation. But *erev brit*, the night before the circumcision, would be the community party in Rachu's home, and the invitation for this was conveyed by phone.

Shaked's *peshta* was held the following Sunday night in the two adjacent apartments in Petah Tikvah where four generations of his family now live. These apartments are connected by a small landing at the top of three flights of stairs in a building just a few blocks off a main highway, convenient for Cochinites from all over Israel to reach by bus or car.

Approximately 70 members of the *kambooLam* crowded into the grandparents' apartment to the left of the landing; from this side a loud babble of Malayalam, Hebrew and English conversation could be heard as far as the street outside, and the air was filled with the familiar aromas of Kerala food. Arriving guests greeted each other with the exclamations of warmth and affection I remembered from parties in the past. In the apartment to the right of the landing, where the traffic was less congested, a few non-Cochinite friends of the young parents were talking quietly. The mother and baby rested in the bedroom there, visited and congratulated for a few moments at a time by individuals or small clusters of guests.

The parlor of the grandparents' apartment was dominated by a long table covered with a white cloth and many plates of colorful fruits and vegetables, an egg and a potato, a citron and its fragrant leaves, and the customary wine and bread. After reciting the usual *Arbith* prayer, about 15 of the older Cochinite men sat down at this beautifully arranged table, while the women, children and younger men squeezed against the walls and filled the dining alcove for the blessing of the fruits. After the men at the table had recited appropriate benedictions and tasted or smelled the various items, they passed them on to the women for their turn.[9]

With this ritual completed, the women began serving snacks and drinks, but the meal could not begin until the men seated at the table had completed a lengthy reading from a set of old books. I later found out these were copies of *Sefer Brit Yitzhak*, a Cochin collection of portions from the Torah, Song of Songs, Prophets, Psalms, Ethics of the Fathers, Mishna and Zohar, including particular references to the *brit mila*.[10] Different passages were being read simultaneously by several of the most learned men. At key points, the baby's father, Aaron, an Iraqi who has adopted many Cochin practices, was instructed about portions which he was to read alone. In Cochin the men would have continued these readings throughout the night, I was told, but in Israel the reading is abbreviated to fit within the framework of the community party. Rachu explained:

> In Cochin we thought it was necessary to stay awake all night to protect the baby. We also used to believe that the child should not be allowed to sleep upside down on his tummy. Now in

[9]According to the late Balfour Salem (3/21/92), in India the prayer for *ishbe b' samim* (fragrant herbs) used to be recited over the leaves of a *thulasi* plant, sacred to Hindus, rather than *etrog* (citron) leaves. These blessings over the fruits and the fragrances are also associated with special prayers during the period of mourning on the Saturday afternoon after a death, he said. Thus we see how particular ritual elements frame the entire cycle of life from birth to death.

[10]*Sefer Brit Itzhak* (Bombay: Lebanon Printing Press, 1909) was compiled and published by Judah David Ashkenazy, a Cochin Jew who was a *mohel* (circumciser) as well as a publisher of Hebrew books. (Katz and Goldberg, 1993, pp. 237-238).

Israel we do not follow all these practices.

As *Sefer Brit Yitzhak* was being read, most of the guests
continued to socialize loudly, munching snacks and helping
themselves to a variety of liquor and soft drinks. At last the men
finished reading and the women placed heaped bowls of rice,
curries and salads on tables in the dining alcove next to the kitchen.
As at previous parties, guests ate buffet-style, standing and
seated wherever they could find a place. And as always, vast
amounts of food were consumed, the liquor continued to flow, and
spirits were high. Despite the continuous uproar, several young
children managed to fall asleep in one of the two small bedrooms.
    Eventually seven toasts were proposed in a unique Paradesi
style—a custom followed in all major parties in Cochin and Israel.[11]
Though I failed to note the details of this custom during the
commotion of several *peshtas*, I have since learned that the eldest
man of the community, called the *kaarnan*,[12] (or the eldest Paradesi
man attending the party) always begins and ends the seven toasts.
He lifts a glass of wine or liquor and chants in a set mixture of
Portuguese, Malayalam and Hebrew words, beginning "Bon Saa-
oodi . . . . ki bi bah" (translated "Good health and long life to . . .")
At an *erev brit* party the seven toasts are proposed in honor of the
following: the newborn boy, the father and mother of the baby, the
circumciser and the godfather, the baby and his grandfather and
grandmother (in Malayalam), the owner of the house, the *kaarnan*
(recited by the guests), and the community (*kahal hakadosh*, "the
holy congregation" in Hebrew). Between each of the toasts, Cochin
Hebrew songs are sung with great enthusiasm.
    After the seventh toast the *birkat hamazon* was recited at the
table, with as many women and men as possible crowded around the
edges, leaning over the shoulders of those who were still seated. All

---

[11]Thanks to Sassoon Roby for the following details on the toasts. He notes that
the toasts are proposed for parties associated with "weddings, circumcisions, bat/
bar mitzvahs, first time when the boy reads Torah or Maftir" (letter, 4/19/93).
    [12]"Kaarnan" is the Paradesi version of the Malayalam term *karanavan*,
referring to the eldest man in a Nayar joint family.

joined in escalating fervor, clapping their hands and singing in full voice the final "Halleluyah odeh". This time the hands of blessing were placed on the heads of Rachu, Ellis and Koko Roby, the grandparents and great-grandmother of the baby. Shaked and his mother remained quietly in the next-door apartment, saving their strength for the events of the following day. In the familiar bustle of spreading out quilts and blankets on beds, sofas and floors, making room for everyone who needed a place to sleep, it seemed to me that little had changed in the more than six years since my last Cochinite party.

Looking back on this occasion, I finally inquired about why Rachu had referred to the party as *"Havdallah rathri"*. Havdallah prayers for ending the Sabbath (or any other holy day) were not actually recited, as the party was on a Sunday night rather than a Saturday evening, but in some ways this *peshta* did incorporate elements from the traditional Cochin Havdallah ritual. Back in Jew Town, there was always a large community gathering on the Saturday night before any circumcision, which included the blessing of the fruits along with a special set of prayers and songs from the Cochin prayer book *Huppat Hatanim*.[13] Then there would be another party on the night before the mila, featuring another blessing of the fruits and the reading of *Sefer Brit Yitzhak*. In fact Rachu did not know precisely what the men were reading at the table once the blessing of the fruits was over; this was not within her realm of expertise. It is in arranging the fruits and other items to be blessed that the women become intimately involved with the ritual, and in this respect the two nights are "exactly the same," she told me.[14]

The following day's *brit mila* celebration, in contrast to the

[13]*Huppat Hatanim* (The Wedding Canopy) is a collection of Cochin Jewish rituals and songs originally published in Amsterdam by J. Props (1757), then edited by Naphtali E.Roby and published in Bombay by Judah David Ashkenazy (1917).

[14]Her practical approach to the ritual is an excellent example of Jewish women's food-centered "sacralization of the feminine", as discussed by Sered, 1992. Investigation is needed to see whether many Cochinite women refer to the condensed *erev brit* party in Israel as "havdallah rathri," even when it is not on a

peshta, was filled with religious and secular rituals which were primarily Israeli, rather than Indian. However it also included some subtle continuities with Cochin practice. In Cochin the baby would have been carried from his home to the synagogue by a childless woman relative, both of them wrapped in a *tallit* (prayer shawl); he would have been carried first to the women's gallery upstairs behind the upper *bimah*, then handed to his father at the door to the women's section, to be carried downstairs to the main part of the synagogue for the actual circumcision. In Israel Shaked's *brit mila* was held in a large *ulam* (hall), rented out to private parties for weddings and other celebrations. Following Cochin tradition, but without any fanfare, he was carried from his apartment to the *ulam* by taxi in the arms of Dr. Essie Sassoon, his mother's unmarried aunt, both of them wrapped together in a *tallit*. At the *ulam* she placed him in a decorated bassinet, and when the time came for the circumcision to be performed, she handed him to his father. Even outsider guests, who outnumbered Cochinites, must have noticed that Dr. Essie was dressed in the traditional Cochin festival dress for women (silk blouse, *lunghi* and shawl decorated with gold sequins), but they probably did not note her role in the ritual. It escaped the attention of the non-Cochinite video cameraman who had been hired to document the celebration.

The order of prayers for the circumcision followed the traditional Cochin prayer book, *Huppat Hatanim*, with a few special prayers and tunes, but in most ways it was similar to any Israeli *brit mila*. A chair was set aside for Eliyahu Hanabi, as is the practice in Cochin and many other Jewish communities. The

---

Saturday. Rachel Roby pointed out to me that for both occasions there must be potatoes and eggs on the table along with the fruits; she did not know why, but she knew the appropriate blessing for them. Balfour Salem saw no religious significance to having eggs and potatoes. "It's just a custom," he said, noting that it is also a Cochinite custom to eat eggs and potatoes every Saturday night after Havdallah, because they can be cooked in a hurry. Katz and Goldberg (1993, p. 238) interpret the eggs and potatoes in Kabbalistic terms as "round foods" identified with mourning and rebirth, served at this point to comfort the newborn child for losing the state of holiness he enjoyed in the womb.

circumcision was carried out by an Ashkenazi rabbi from Binyamina who is friendly with the community and performs most of their life-cycle rituals.

After the circumcision, the guests sorted themselves out at the elaborately set tables. Most of the Cochinites sat together, with other tables occupied by friends of Shaked's parents from the Army (where they had met) and from their places of work, neighbors, and colleagues from the banks where Shaked's grandparents work. The meal was an elaborate one, completely Western in menu and style of serving. An Israeli master of ceremonies and a clown provided entertainment, all in Hebrew, introducing the families and encouraging everyone to dance to the popular music which dominated the after-dinner atmosphere. Finally the music stopped, the emcee and the clown left, the waiters began clearing off tables and the non-Cochinite guests departed.

With some difficulty the video cameraman had to be persuaded to stay for the *birkat hamazon* and the "Halleluyah Odeh" blessing which followed it. This time the chant reached its climax with Rachu placing her hand on the head of the baby, and all who could reach them blessing the heads of the new parents. Tears mixed with laughter and ululation as the last notes of the song were drawn out. A copy of the video was sent to Cochin, where all the *kambooLam* remaining in Jew Town could see their newest member surrounded by all their relations and friends, and where they too could join in the blessing.

Outsiders and Insiders:
Public and Community Rituals

An outsider to the Cochinite community, attending the portion of a life-cycle event which is held in an *ulam*, or noting the way community members are outnumbered in the Binyamina synagogue, might suspect that the Paradesi community is fast assimilating or being "absorbed" into whatever mainstream there is in contemporary Israeli culture. Following this line of thought, their public and more "Israeli" ritual events might be expected eventually to overshadow or even replace their home-based parties. But it is not necessary to view older and newer forms of a ritual event as competing for ascendance. In a study emphasizing foodways Theophano (1991) shows how two very different wedding feasts both demonstrated ethnic continuity in an Italian-American family—one a traditional buffet with Italian foods and the other a formal sit-down meal with "English" (non-Italian) foods.

Neither is an assimilation or "absorption" model the only way to understand change in Jewish custom and ritual (Weingrod 1985:ix-xix). My approach in this paper is closer to the performance model used by Weingrod (1990) in his portrayal of a new *Hillula* ritual created by North African Jews in Beersheba, and by Goldstein (1985) in her discussion of Iranian-Israeli "definitional ceremonies." Along with Cernea's (1988) symbolic analysis of a new *Hillula* ceremony in Washington, D.C., these studies stress continuity with the past in creating new ritual forms.

After twelve years of involvement with the Cochin Paradesi community in Israel, I predict that their home-based parties will continue along with their Israeli-style *ulam* and synagogue events, for the two styles of "performance" are not fundamentally in conflict. On the contrary, their participation in a set of associated community and public rituals reflects continuity with their traditional practice in Kerala, and not a move away from it.

Through this evolving set of parallel rituals in Israel, Cochinites continue the bicultural balancing act they accomplished so gracefully in South India. Back in Cochin, for example, Jewish marriages were traditionally celebrated with eight days of community rituals and parties, most of them held in various homes in Jew Town. But part of each ritual sequence also involved hospitality to non-Paradesis, for the wedding ceremony itself (held in the synagogue) and for a special party afterward. Likewise, Simchat Torah was both the high point of the Jewish religious year and also the holiday on which the synagogue was open to outsiders. As recalled by Ruby Daniel:

[On Simchat Torah] many gentiles came to see the synagogue

decorated with lights and garlands of jasmine.... All the [Jewish] men and the ladies.... went from one synagogue to the other to kiss the Torah.... Usually the members of one synagogue did not visit the others except on this occasion (Daniel and Johnson 1995).

During their many centuries of life in Cochin, Jews operated in a very Indian fashion as a caste among castes—one *jati* among many in the complex fabric of Kerala society. Relations among castes involve an elaborate system of reciprocal economic and political exchanges, interlaced with mutual attendance at ritual events. Through accepting and returning ritual hospitality and appropriate gifts, good relations are maintained with employers and employees, business associates and customers, political officials and neighbors from many different castes and classes. Feasts associated with weddings and other life-cycle rituals provide conspicuous occasions for such exchange (Appadurai 1981:504-505). In hosting huge and elaborate feasts for guests from many castes, the Jews in Cochin were doing just what almost any Kerala family would have to do, especially those in the middle to upper classes.[15]

Reminiscing about Cochin wedding celebrations when she was young, Ruby Daniel writes:

Usually on the day after the [Jewish] wedding, there is a party for non-Jews who are also invited to celebrate the marriage. These include friends of the bride and bridegroom and of their families, sometimes the tenants who lived on the land owned by the families, and sometimes important guests such as officials. The guests bring presents, some say according to the grandeur of the wedding. ... On that day food is cooked specially for non-Jewish guests. Hindus have a Hindu cook,

[15]For a similar analysis of Jewish and Muslim weddings in North Africa, see Valensi (1989), who notes that Tunisian Jews traditionally invited their Muslim neighbors to participate in certain important ritual events associated with the ten-day wedding cycle.

because they won't eat meat or fish or egg. Christians have Christian cooks and victuals of their own kind. They are also rich high class people and are so treated (Daniel and Johnson 1995).

There is no problem regarding *kashrut* at a Kerala wedding, I was assured in 1981 by Cochin Jewish friends who took me to a large Indian Christian wedding and reception in Ernakulam. They steered me through throngs of guests, past tables overflowing with forbidden delicacies to the vegetarian section where Jews knew it was safe to eat. Any feast in which meat is served (whether by Jews, Christians, Muslims or non-vegetarian Hindu castes) will also include a full vegetarian menu prepared by Brahmin cooks, guaranteed to contain nothing that would violate high-caste Hindu or Jewish dietary laws. Members of different castes attending the same ritual event are expected to sit separately and eat different foods, but all are participating in an ongoing cultural system which reinforces their social bonds. Meeting the cultural and personal needs of each guest is an important part of the hospitality.

The same analysis may be applied to the portion of any life-cycle ritual which takes place in an Israeli *ulam*. Whereas in Kerala the "outsiders" to the community were non-Jewish friends and acquaintances, in Israel it is non-Indians who can be seen as "outsiders" incorporated into community celebrations such as weddings and circumcisions. Non-Cochinites invited to an *ulam* event include the familiar categories of friends, neighbors, associates from work and "important" guests such as the supervisors or employers of various family members. To ensure their comfort by providing familiar Israeli foods, rituals and entertainment is not a sign of Paradesi assimilation into Israeli culture, any more than the providing of ritually appropriate foods for different castes was a sign of losing their Jewish identity in Cochin. Indian foods, rituals and entertainment at such public events would be unfamiliar to non-Indian guests—violating the unwritten rules of making guests comfortable—but these Indian foods and rituals are not being lost. They are still preserved in the *peshta.*

Internal Community Solidarity

As Barbara Myerhoff states so aptly, "It is their very nature for rituals to establish continuity" (1978:108), and it is critically important in times of drastic social change to create rituals which link the old world with the new. Paradesi parties in Israel do this very effectively. In a *peshta*, the Cochinites piece together customs from their Kerala past with new Israeli ways of celebrating; they reassert the definition of their community as they state its central values in ritual form.

Keeping in close personal contact with each other and with the larger community of Cochinites is a primary objective which is much more difficult to carry out in Israel than it was in Cochin. They must create occasions on which it will happen. Parties draw together members of the *kambooLam* from all parts of Israel, reminding them of the strength of their numbers and of their commitment to one another. The cycle of reciprocity played out in the parties stresses the responsibility of each member and household for the whole group. As Essie Ashkenazy and Koko Roby explained to me during a rare break when they were resting from their cooking for a party: "We have to do all this. We must return for the parties others have given"(6/28/81).

The old and the new are skilfully combined in structuring a party so that it "feels like Cochin" but is viable in Israel. The people are familiar—the most important ingredient in the party. Most of the core group of "Jew Town folks" are on hand and they remember and talk about how things were done in Cochin. Most of the food consists of typical Kerala dishes. The prayers and blessings are all from Cochin, as are customs like "egging" on Simchat Torah. New touches from the Israeli scene include some foods, popular music, dancing and party games.

Accommodations must be made to the practical constraints of their Israeli life, as in their shifting of some religious rituals from the synagogue to the home. In 1981, Simchat Torah—an essentially synagogue-based religious holiday—extended into the home-based party format of the *peshta*. The precious songs which used to be sung in the synagogue courtyard, and which are unique to Cochin Jewry, were now at the center of that party. The time was evening rather than afternoon, and the setting was a crowded apartment in Binyamina. No, it wasn't the same, but the community was there together, and the history and spirit represented in the songs continued.

In the past decade parties have continued to evolve in creative and flexible ways. The Shingli songs for Simchat Torah have been restored to their original place in the afternoon *Mincha* service. I imagine that the larger size of the Koders' new house in Binyamina and its proximity to the synagogue also must affect the form of the evening Simchat Torah parties which they continue to host. During a recent brief visit to Israel, I was entertained with videotapes of several *peshtas* which I had missed. The Robys in Petah Tikvah have begun holding parties outdoors (weather permitting); they set up rented chairs and tables and colored lights in the area beneath and behind their apartment building, near where they usually build their *succah*. Other elements of the party seem to be unchanged.

The introduction of rented video recording equipment has added an element of conscious reflexivity to the proceedings, especially when the camera is operated by a community member who captures specifically Indian details of both an evening *peshta* and the wedding or circumcision which follows it the next day. Videos are enjoyed again and again, with attention to each detail and with an eye to preserving memories for future generations. Mailing these tapes to friends and relatives in Cochin adds an immediacy to the sense of connection with Jew Town.

The institution of the community party serves as a socializing ritual which profoundly affects membership in the group. Children grow up looking forward to these gatherings, being thoroughly included in them, and learning from them unspoken lessons in what it means to be a Cochinite. They see enacted such values as familiarity with Indian food and religious ritual, responsibility for the group, and the ability to relax and have a good time. Some everyday norms are temporarily suspended, or rather stretched to a different shape. Drinking and pranks are expected on these occasions, but implicit rules limit such behavior, rules which can be learned only by participation. The same socialization process goes on with newcomers who are welcomed into the community through invitations to parties. Boundaries of Cochinite community are defined and redefined through the *peshtas*, both by attendance at parties and by the events and style which characterize them.

Myerhoff reminds us that rituals are "paradoxical and dangerous enterprises" because they are artificially constructed, "yet designed to suggest the inevitability and absolute truth of their messages" (1978:86). When participants become aware of themselves as having created a ritual, they may hover on the brink of "impending foolishness," the awareness that all culture is invented (1984, 1986). Something of this discomfort was reflected in frequent remarks that Simchat Torah in Binyamina is "nothing" compared to celebrations in Cochin. A similar skepticism was expressed to me in 1981 by a young Paradesi woman who had recently arrived from Cochin. As we worked together cutting onions for a *peshta* chicken curry, she mused:

> The older Cochinites carry on a make-believe life in Israel, trying to do things exactly the same here as they did in Cochin. They try to make the festivals the same here, but they can't be the same. When they have big parties like this, it is trying to carry on the way things were in Jew Town at festival time, singing and dancing and all. But the next generation won't continue doing all this. I won't continue it, doing all this cooking and preparation (6/28/81).

Another young woman expressed similar reservations about the parties, pointing to ways in which they are different from parties in Cochin. But on further discussion with both of them, it became clear that they expect the *peshtas* themselves to continue.

"All this cooking" they saw as unnecessary—and no wonder, given their heavy work schedules. They favored a trend toward potluck dinners, where the work of preparing Kerala food would be shared by many women. But the parties themselves will continue, they agreed, even if their form is changed.

Surely this is the nature of ritual, continually changing to meet new circumstances. It takes us to the edge of formlessness, where we see that our lives may have no inherent structure, then provides a path back from the brink, as we humans create again and again the forms which express our particular values and shape the continuity of our lives (Myerhoff 1986). For Cochinites in Israel, the values and continuity of *namoDe kambooLam* are reinforced again and again when they come together for the prayers, songs, laughter and food at each community party.

Sources cited

Abraham, Margaret. 1989. "Ethnic Identity and Marginality: A Study of the Jews of India." Unpublished Ph.D. dissertation, Syracuse University.

Appadurai, Arjun. 1981. "Gastro-Politics in Hindu South Asia," *American Ethnologist* 8(3):494-511.

Areshet Sefatenu. 1979. Ashdod, Israel: Shomer Israel Synagogue.

Brown, Linda Keller, and Mussell, Kay, eds. 1985. *Ethnic and Regional Foodways in the United States.* Knoxville: University of Tennessee Press.

Cernea, Ruth. 1988. "Flaming Prayers: Hillula in a New Home," pp. 162-191 in J. Kugelmass, ed., *Between Two Worlds: Ethnographic Essays on American Jewry.* Ithaca: Cornell University Press.

Daniel, Ruby, with Barbara C. Johnson. 1995. *Long Ago in Malabar: Memories of a Cochin Jewish Woman.* Philadelphia: The Jewish Publication Society. Forthcoming.

Goldstein, Judith L. 1985. "Iranian Ethnicity in Israel: The Performance of Identity," pp. 237-257 in Alex Weingrod, ed., *Studies in Israeli Ethnicity: After the Ingathering.* New York:

Gordon and Breach.

Johnson, Barbara C. 1975. "Shingli or Jewish Cranganore in the Traditions of the Cochin Jews of India." Unpublished M.A. thesis, Smith College.

————. 1985. "'Our Community' in Two Worlds: The Cochin Paradesi Jews in India and Israel." Unpublished Ph.D. dissertation, University of Massachusetts.

————. 1995. "Cochin Jews and Kaifeng Jews: Reflections on Caste, Patrilineage, Community and Conversion," in Jonathan Goldstein, ed., *Jewish Diasporas in India and China: Comparative and Historical Perspectives.* Forthcoming. Hebrew version in *Pe'amim,* vol. 60, forthcoming.

Kalcik, Susan. 1985. "Ethnic Foodways in Amercia: Symbol and the Performance of Identity," pp. 37-65 in L.K. Brown and K. Mussell, eds. *Ethnic and Regional Foodways in the United States.* Knoxville: University of Tennessee Press.

Katz, Nathan, and Ellen S. Goldberg. 1993. *The Last Jews of Cochin: Jewish Identity in Hindu India.* Columbia: University of South Carolina Press.

Kushner, Gilbert. 1973. *Immigrants from India in Israel: Planned Change in an Administered Community.* Tucson: University of Arizona Press.

Moskowitz, Stuart B. 1986. "The Cochini Transformed: Emerging Ethnic Identity among South Indian Jews in Israel." Unpublished Ph.D. dissertation, Catholic University of America.

Myerhoff, Barbara. 1978. *Number Our Days.* New York: Simon and Schuster.

————. 1984. "Number Our Days: The Aging and their Search for Meaning." Smith College lecture.

————. 1986. " 'Life Not Death in Venice': Its Second Life," pp. 261-288 in V. Turner and E. Bruner, eds., *The Anthropology of Experience.* Urbana: University of Illinois Press.

Sered, Susan. 1988. "Food and Holiness: Cooking as a Sacred Act Among Middle-Eastern Women." *Anthropological Quarterly* 61(3):129-139.

————. 1992. *Women as Ritual Experts: The Religious Lives*

of Elderly Jewish Women in Jerusalem. New York and Oxford: Oxford University Press.

Shokeid, Moshe. 1971. "Moshav Sela: Frustration and Crisis in the Process of Absorption," pp. 103-124 in Ovadia Shapiro, ed., *Rural Settlements of New Immigrants in Israel.* Rehovot: Settlement Study Center.

Weingrod, Alex, ed. 1985. "Introduction," pp. ix-xix in *Studies in Israeli Ethnicity: After the Ingathering.* New York: Gordon and Breach.

—————— . 1990. *The Saint of Beersheba.* Albany: S.U.N.Y. Press.

Valensi, Lucette. 1989. "Religious Orthodoxy or Local Tradition: Marriage Celebration in Southern Tunisia," pp. 65-84 in M.R. Cohen and A.L. Udovitch, eds., *Jews Among Arabs: Contacts and Boundaries.* Princeton, NJ: Darwin Press.

Theophano, Janet. 1991. "'I Gave Him a Cake': An Interpretation of Two Italian-American Weddings," pp. 44-54 in S. Stern and J.A. Cicala, eds., *Creative Ethnicity: Symbols and Strategies of Contemporary Ethnic Life.* Logan: Utah State University Press.

Walerstein, Marcia S. 1987. "Public Rituals Among the Jews from Cochin, India, in Israel: Expressions of Ethnic Identity." Unpublished Ph.D. dissertation, University of California at Los Angeles.

Part II

The Bene Israel

3

The Bene Israel Villagers of Kolaba District: Generations, Culture Change, Changing Identities

Shirley Berry Isenberg

This is essentially a narrative about Bene Israel villagers, tracing the evolution of change in basic characteristics descriptive of Bene Israel identity. In the eighteenth century I doubt that it ever occurred to a Bene Israel to verbalize in so many words as to how he or she would describe the essentials of Bene Israel identity. However, even though the facts about the Bene Israel of that period are sketchy, we can, with good reason, arrive at a depiction of eighteenth century Bene Israel as being a thoroughly Indian endogamous entity of villagers located within an area identifiable as Kolaba District.[1] The Bene Israel were distinguishable from their neighbors only because of certain Bene Israel specifically Jewish observances. They were living in isolation from mainstream Jewry. They were uneducated and illiterate. Their traditional occupation was oil-pressing, but they were also engaged in agriculture, peddling and carpentry. This paper will show how and why in the nineteenth century the Bene Israel were exposed simultaneously to two entirely separate and non-indigenous processes which, gradually but inevitably, brought the Bene Israel into mainstream Judaism and also led them away from village life. Totally new Bene Israel patterns of identity developed.

---

[1]Kolaba (or Kulaba) District of Maharashtra State, India was designated as such by the British. (Today it has been renamed as Raigad District.) To its north lie Greater Bombay and Thana District. It stretches 160 miles southward along the Arabian Sea as far as the mouth and extent of the Savitri River; and 40 to 60 miles eastward from the Arabian Sea to the border of Poona District and the foothills of the Western Ghats.

The following narrative is addressed especially to students of ethnology, religion, and Jewish history because:

1) There are virtually no more Bene Israel today in their native villages, yet the family histories of the now elderly Bene Israel who were born and lived most of their lives in villages of Kolaba District are the principal links to generations past. Recording as many as possible of their memories is therefore an urgent priority.

2) Conclusive documentation as to pre-seventeenth century Bene Israel history has not yet been discovered, although inferential reasoning leaves no doubt in my mind that the Bene Israel formed a separate, vestigially Jewish entity in the Konkan[2] for at least several centuries preceding the seventeenth century (Isenberg:24-37).

3) No one has as yet undertaken the difficult but intriguing challenge to search systematically for pre-seventeenth century definitive documentation about the Bene Israel, not to mention a search for more documents about the seventeenth century itself. This search should begin not only with the histories of those villages where Bene Israel are known to have been born, but also with the histories of numerous additional Kolaba District villages which are indicated by Bene Israel traditional locative surnames.

4) Nor has anyone as yet begun the even more complicated venture of coordinating a thorough search of pre-eighteenth century archives and official records of all sorts located in or about the entire Konkan—especially in the

---

[2]Kolaba District is part of the Konkan central coastal strip of western India. The Konkan extends from about 50 miles north of Bombay southward as far as Goa. Since this paper concentrates on Bene Israel villagers, and because the area of Bene Israel rural settlement is demarcated by the boundaries of Kolaba District, and not of the Konkan as a whole, I prefer to emphasize the area of their village roots. Such places as Bombay, Greater Bombay and Thana, which are not part of Kolaba District, are places where those Bene Israel who migrated to them quickly lost their identity as villagers.

domains of the Ahmednagar and Bijapur Sultanates in the fifteenth and sixteenth centuries, and in the Sidi territories of the Nawabs of Janjira, or from the annals of Shivaji (1627-1680)—in an attempt to spot whatever documentation may still be extant about the Bene Israel and their antecedents. This avenue of research would require alerting many different scholars who are already working on such documents in the local languages and in medieval variants of those languages, arranging with them to watch for and point out any reference to Jews or "Israelites" or Shanwar Telis (see below), or references to Jewish customs. The name "Bene Israel" may not have designated this group in earlier times.

It may not be obvious, but the above-mentioned four factors do hang together.

Until the twentieth century the villages and towns of Kolaba District comprised the native heartland of the Bene Israel, i.e. where their parents, or grandparents, or great-grandparents had been born and lived all or much of their lives, where some family members were still living in the old homestead, and where those who no longer lived there returned (or would have liked to return) to celebrate together the Jewish Holidays and family rites of passage. However, the "heartland" reality and sentiment slowly faded away. In brief, this is how it happened.

The British East India Company had moved its headquarters from Surat (in Gujarat) to "the Islands of Bombay" in 1674, whereupon the natural harbor and the few fishing villages on these islands quickly mushroomed into the busy port and metropolis of Bombay to which, by the second half of the eighteenth century hundreds of Bene Israel and thousands of others were attracted. They left their village or small town existence seeking the opportunities for employment and education that Bombay offered, or to enlist in the Native Forces of the British East India Company's (later the British Government's) military services. The Company recruited large numbers of Bene Israel volunteers not only from Bombay but also from the countryside as early as 1750. In the eighteenth century the Company records refer to the Bene Israel enlistments as belonging to "the native Jew caste". However, the Bene Israel did not refer to themselves as "Jew" or "Yehudi". To the Bene Israel the terms "Jew" and "Yehudi" referred especially to Baghdadi and other Arabic-speaking Jews who settled in Bombay with their families, mainly in the early years of the nineteenth century.

In the military cantonments there were quarters for one's wife and children. Here not only the enlisted men but also their wives and children received an elementary education. Bene Israel enlisted men rose to the highest ranks possible for native soldiers, way out of proportion to their numbers when compared with promotions of Indians of other religions, sub-castes, etc. Many Bene Israel received medals for bravery and outstanding service in the field of battle. Bene Israel were also in the Company's so-called Marine Battalion. And, from the areas of the Konkan under non-British rule, there are a few *sanads*[3] known to us which testify that some Bene Israel in the eighteenth century held a high rank in the Angrey-Maratha fleet.

Many Bene Israel migrants from villages settled in Bombay and found work in the construction of buildings and in the shipyards, a few as contractors, many as carpenters. Rarely did they set up businesses of their own. The building and carpentry skills they had brought with them from their villages, but in Bombay they learned more modern techniques and were introduced to new kinds of implements, etc. They did not pursue the traditional Bene Israel specialization as oil-pressers because in Bombay they found that this essential occupation was already in the hands of other traditionally oil-presser groups.

Throughout the eighteenth century most Bene Israel were still living in Kolaba District, typically with very few Bene Israel per village. Each family owned a few acres of land (only a few Bene

---

[3] *Sanad:* Indian term for an official government document or warrant containing a title to land or to an office; or a privilege or authorization for something specific to be done.

Israel had large landholdings), a few cattle and chickens, a house which often sheltered three generations of the family together and to which rooms were added as the extended family grew. There would be an oil-press, one or two bullocks, and a two-wheel wooden bullock-cart which the head of the family would use seasonally to peddle in nearby small towns his surplus, if any, of agricultural produce (rice, coconuts, mangoes, firewood, edible oils, and oil for lamp-light). Bene Israel were known as *Shanwar Teli* (Saturday oilmen) because no Bene Israel would process or sell oil on the Sabbath. During the eighteenth century even in the towns there were not more than a hundred Bene Israel persons living in any one place. There was very little of what could be called Bene Israel community life. Even so, we can refer to the Bene Israel as a community because of their strict endogamy and the particular Jewish observances which they shared. Tradition has it that before the eighteenth century (no one knows when), the Bene Israel were "discovered" by a Jew called David Rahabi who identified them as Jews when he learned of their Jewish practices: namely that they observed the Sabbath by doing no manner of work, nor did they kindle any fire or cook on the Sabbath; they recited, in Hebrew, the opening lines of the *Shema*[4] on every occasion for rituals or prayer; they practised circumcision of their male infants on the eighth day after birth; and they refused to eat any fish that did not have fins and scales. After Rahabi had observed these customs among them, he chose three young Bene Israel men from three different families, gave them instruction in Judaism and some *Halacha*,[5] taught them to read and write (but not to translate) Hebrew, and had them copy his books—presumably the five books of Moses or parts of them and some Jewish holiday liturgies. These men were known as Kazis, and it was their duty to travel among

---

[4]*Shema* (Hebrew): Literally "Hear!". The *Shema* is a passage from Deuteronomy 6:4-9 which expresses the fundamental tenet of the Jewish faith, beginning with "Hear, O Israel, the Lord our God, the Lord is One."

[5]*Halacha* (Hebrew): Traditional law; civil and ritual Jewish law and custom for which there is no explicit instruction in the Pentateuch, but which is accepted as Rabbinic traditional law.

Bene Israel families throughout Kolaba District, administering according to Jewish law all rites of passage and other Jewish rituals, judging disputes among Bene Israel, and teaching Jewish prayers by rote. The title, honors, and duties of being a *Kazi* were inherited from father to son descending from the three original *Kazis*. Whatever group prayer and rituals were to be performed took place at one's home.[6] There were no Bene Israel synagogues or prayer halls until the establishment in Bombay of the first Bene Israel synagogue in 1796. This synagogue came into being through the inspiration, efforts and money of Native Commandant Samaji Hassaji (Samuel Ezekiel) Divekar after he had been released from being a prisoner-of-war of the Muslim Sultan of Mysore (see Isenberg:314-324). Samaji's father, Hassaji, was the second Bene Israel to have settled in Bombay (Kehimkar:78). All three of Hassaji's sons enlisted on the Native Army of the British East India Company.

We read of some Bene Israel women still (in the late eighteenth and early nineteenth centuries) secretly offering petitionary prayers to idols of Hindu deities who were believed to have the power to ward off evil and disease. And, as all Jews in all parts of the Diaspora have done and continue to do, so too the Bene Israel incorporated into their life-cycle rituals many customs as performed by their non-Jewish neighbors, customs which in no way contradict tenets of Judaism but which were and are in vogue among the local non-Jews—in this case, among the Hindus and Muslims in Kolaba District.

Particularly fascinating is the fact that the Bene Israel today as well as in the past feel a special affinity with the Prophet Elijah. They invoke his presence and/or help chiefly during a specific Bene Israel ritual called the Malida ceremony, which is performed in connection with certain rites of passage, or with the making and fulfilment of vows. Although some features of this ceremony are reminiscent of a specific Jewish, Muslim or Hindu custom, the

---

[6]For a more detailed account of Bene Israel life in the eighteenth century, see Isenberg, pp. 49-56.

complex as a whole is unique to the Bene Israel (see Isenberg:111-117).

In the eighteenth century there was some Bene Israel mobility other than to Bombay, or to various stations during military service. It happened because of the frequent warfare in those days. In its wake armed gangs, and also pirates coming from the sea, would indiscriminately pillage and burn village homesteads.[7] The afflicted families would move for safety— usually eastward,[8] either finding some niche in some eastern village, or by founding a new village. And this is why we find Bene Israel with village-linked surnames being born and living their lives, even in the eighteenth century, in villages with names other than the name of their ancestral village.

It is important to understand why village-linked[9] Bene Israel surnames are significant. Even in the twentieth century, whether in India, Israel, Canada, Australia, England or other countries of their current Diaspora, every Bene Israel still knows his other "kar" family name. In a synagogue when a Bene Israel is called either to read from the Torah[10] or to recite blessings over it, his Bene Israel surname is mentioned together with his Hebrew name. "Kar" is the locative suffix attached to the name of one's ancestral village which, more often than not, is no longer the name of the place where one's father was born. But it is the name of the village in Kolaba District where centuries ago one's paternal ancestors were born and lived. The late Benjamin Jacob Israel (Wargharkar) has researched many aspects of his Bene Israel community, and he has identified 135 Bene Israel surnames, all of which are attributable to specific villages within Kolaba District (see Israel: 120-166 and Isenberg: 156-159, 368-373).

[7]There was, in this, no anti-Jewish element whatsoever.

[8]But not quite as far eastward as the foothills of the north-south mountain range and, therefore, still within the area of the Kolaba District.

[9]This term "village-linked" includes not only villages, but also what are today towns, such as Ashtami, Chaul, Roha and Shriwardhan.

[10]*Torah* (Hebrew): The Five Books of Moses: Genesis, Exodus, Leviticus, Numbers, and Deuteronomy.

In order to learn more than we now know about the past history of the Bene Israel, a concerted effort should be made in as many as possible of these Bene Israel surname-linked villages to find out whatever is known or recorded which is in any way relevant to Bene Israel residence in that place; and to find out when that particular village was founded. Whatever village records are still extant might reveal references to its former Bene Israel residents. Other sources would be the local keepers of genealogies (important in India), the local legends, written and oral accounts of historical events especially of pre-British rulers. All such information would help the historian in orienting, dating, describing, and proving a Bene Israel presence in Kolaba District possibly much earlier than the seventeenth century.

We do know just how, during the second quarter of the nineteenth century, two radical changes entered the lives of rural a well as of urban Bene Israel, changes stimulated by two faiths, Christian and Jewish, creating new priorities and, consequently, new identities.

Not only in Bombay but throughout Kolaba District various Christian missionary societies, in the hope of converting Indians to Christianity, set up several free schools, making available to Indian children (Hindu, Muslim, Jewish and Christian alike) a knowledge of the English language, and affording them a secular as well as a Christian education. And, more or less simultaneously, several dedicated Jewish teachers, mainly from Cochin, and *Hazanim*[11] came to the Konkan in order to introduce to the Bene Israel synagogue worship, synagogue administration, actual Torah scrolls,[12] and the full range of *Halacha*.[13] The impact of these two forces upon the subsequent history of the Bene Israel was fundamental and irreversible. For the purposes of this article, only

---

[11]*Hazan* (Hebrew): The cantor who chants the liturgy and leads the prayers in a synagogue.

[12]The five Books of Moses written by hand on parchment, rolled and encased either in richly embroidered cloth (the custom of Ashkenazi Jews) or in a wooden case often overlaid with decorations in silver (the Sephardi custom).

[13]Including many actual details to be observed in everyday life.

their relevance to the Bene Israel heartland (not to Bombay and elsewhere) will be discussed here.

The following Table, reporting only about the schools of the American Mission in Kolaba District for the year 1829, appeared in *The Oriental Christian Spectator*, Volume 1, No. 4, April 1830, p. 113.

TABLE 1 : SCHEDULE OF THE NATIVE FREE SCHOOLS, BOYS

Places caste	Teacher's	Girls	Hindoos	Moohum-mudans	Jews	Chris-tians	Total
T'hull	Jew	13	76	4	3	-	83
Allebag	Jew	10	65	10	14	-	89
Nagaum	Jew	15	70	-	17	-	87
Revadunda	Jew	6	79	3	27	1	110
Rohay	Jew	-	43	5	4	-	52
Parlee	Bramhun	-	45	15	-	-	60
Nagoatnay	Bramhun	2	86	2	2	-	90
Pane	Jew	3	56	-	12	-	68
Panwell	Jew	10	61	11	17	-	89
Joonnur	Weaver	2	59	3	-	-	62
Mahim	Maratha	-	30	9	-	-	39
B No. 1	Tailor	-	50	3	-	-	53
O No. 2	Weaver	2	24	1	2	2	29
M No. 3	Bramhun	4	50	-	2	5	57
B No. 4 A	Bramhun	1	51	4	-	-	55
Y No. 5	Bramhun	2	45	5	-	-	50
Mazagaum	Purbhoo	2	35	3	-	-	38
Allebag	Jew H.S.	6	-	-	30	-	30

I do not know where the teachers had been "educated"; possibly either in cantonment schools, or (except for those who were Brahmins) segregated at the rear of the schoolroom in village schools traditionally conducted by and for Brahmins. There were also Native Free Schools conducted by missionaries for girls only, but, as can be seen in the above Table, a few girls were also in attendance in the boys' schools. When one realizes how infinitesimally small was the percentage of Bene Israel compared with percentages of other Indian groups in Kolaba District, the high proportion of Bene Israel in attendance at schools (as shown in the above Table as well as in records of other mission schools) is very impressive. Also, at a time when female literacy worldwide was very low, Bene Israel girls from villages were learning to read and write in three languages: Marathi, English and Hebrew. The 1829 Report mentions that some classes were "under the instruction of Jewish teachers who not only disallow the obser-vance of heathenish customs in their schools, but also manifest considerable interest in giving religious instruction to their pupils." The only high school of the American Mission was in Alibag where all thirty of its male pupils, and probably the six girls too, were Jews. There were many Bene Israel and no Baghdadi or other Jewish families then living in Alibag and other villages of Kolaba District, so we can assume that all Jewish pupils of these mission schools, with the possible exception of the schools in Bombay, were Bene Israel.

The Bene Israel were of special interest to the Rev John Wilson of the Church of Scotland (later the Free Church of Scotland). He lived in Bombay and worked with the people of Bombay and of Kolaba District from the time of his arrival in India in 1829 until his death in 1875. He was a remarkable man, a scholar and an erudite writer on theology, philosophy, various religions, linguistics, and Indian archaeology. He served as President of the Bombay branch of the Royal Asiatic Society for seven years. He was one of the founders of Bombay University (1857) and was Vice Chancellor of Bombay University during 1860-1870. He introduced Hebrew as a subject for matriculation and for higher examinations. Wilson saw in the Bene Israel the Biblical "remnant of Israel" and wrote that "their situation, if properly explained to the Hindus among whom they dwell might facilitate the illustration of the Prophetical testimony to the truth of the Scriptures."[14] In 1836 Wilson arranged for a Census of the Bene Israel to be taken. He

[14]*The Oriental Christian Spectator* 11/1, January 1840, p. 35.

found that there were then "about 8,000 Bene Israel in Bombay and the adjoining territories" (i.e. Kolaba District). He wrote the first substantial account of the Bene Israel and their customs and read this account, in two parts, before the Bombay branch of the Royal Asiatic Society in 1838 and 1839; he also published a long abstract of it in the journal of which he was editor, *The Oriental Christian Spectator*.[15] Much of the information in Wilson's account was incorporated later by H.S.Kehimkar in his History of the Bene-Israel of India, written in 1897 (but not published until 1937, posthumously, and which is the source about pre-twentieth century Bene Israel.

Rev Wilson established many Scottish Mission schools in Kolaba District and in Bombay, some in the English medium and some in the vernacular; one school was for Bene Israel pupils only, but the others were attended by pupils from a variety of different religions as well as by Bene Israel. Wilson's upper schools and College were situated in Bombay. Hebrew was taught in some of Wilson's schools. Wilson had perfected his own knowledge of Hebrew by taking intensive lessons in Bombay from Rabbi David D'Beth Hillel. In 1831 Wilson wrote and published in Bombay *A Grammar of the Hebrew Language, with Points* (i.e. the Hebrew vowels) *in Murathee*, explaining in a pre-publication announcement:

"This Grammar is intended for the benefit of the Native Israelites. . . . In addition to an explanation, and an exemplification of the different parts of speech, it will contain an account of the Creation, the Fall, and the Flood, the Ten Commandments, Selected Moral Sentences, and passages relating to the Messiah contained in the Old Testament, and contrasted with the corresponding ones in the New, both in the Hebrew and Murathee[16] languages, so as to form a set of useful

[15]This Abstract is reproduced in full in Isenberg, pp. 327-338.

[16]Marathi is the language spoken in the Konkan and throughout the State of Maharashtra.

and constructive exercises."[17]

Using this Grammar as a beginning, some of Wilson's pupils became very proficient in Hebrew and in due course became teachers of Hebrew not only in Wilson's schools but also at the college level. These Bene Israel scholars translated from Hebrew into Marathi and they published many Hebrew classical writings, each together with its translation into Marathi, thus giving the Bene Israel access to the Jewish literary heritage.

A Bene Israel, Ezekiel Joseph Rajpurkar, became Superintendent of Schools of the Free Church of Scotland Mission, for all their schools in Bombay and Kolaba District. His son, Joseph Ezekiel Rajpurkar (1834-1905), after studying under the Christian missionaries Rev Wilson, Dr J. M. Mitchell, and Rev R. Nesbit, served as assistant teacher in the Baghdadi (Jewish) David Sassoon Benevolent Institution's school in 1860. After five years he became its headmaster, a position he held for forty years. In 1871 he became Examiner in Hebrew at Bombay University, and in 1876 Additional Examiner in Arts; in 1879 he was appointed a Fellow of Bombay University. Other Bene Israel graduates from Wilson's schools, who hailed from Kolaba District villages as well as from cities, also became teachers and school principals; and many others became medical doctors, advocates, surveyors, engineers, nurses, social welfare workers, civil servants, clerks, etc.

With the establishment of mission schools throughout Kolaba District came the need for a translation of the Bible into the Marathi language and script. As Benjamin J. Israel has so well observed, the missionary translation not only enabled the Bene Israel to read the Bible themselves, but the missionary approach to the Bible

"profoundly influenced the Bene Israel attitude to the Bible, which, for better or worse, differed materially from that of the Orthodox Oriental Jew. They taught them to regard the plain text of the Bible as a self-sufficient guide in matters of religion

[17]Quoted from a pre-publication announcement of the book. *The Oriental Christian Spectator* 2/7, July 1831, p. 9.

and to rely on their own individual reading of the Bible to learn God's law. And, ever since, although the Bene Israel have professed to accept rabbinical teaching and law like their fellow Jews elsewhere, they have never given rabbinical teaching the attention it received elsewhere." (Israel:68).

The mission schools did not make many converts among the Bene Israel. As regards the Scottish mission schools, as late as 1854 after Rev Wilson had been trying for twenty-five years, he admitted that he had not converted a single Bene Israel (see Isenberg:82). In oral and written accounts, a touching and unsophisticated theme recurs in connection with the average Bene Israel's inability to refute specific missionary arguments with Biblical quotations as to why Bene Israel should convert to Christianity. The Bene Israel would reply that he himself was not learned enough, but that there were Jewish scholars who could surely refute the Christian argu-ments. Or, as Rev J. Henry Lord, a missionary of the Anglican Church, forty years later wrote: "with a large number of them [Bene Israel] Christianity does not seem to be wrong for any other reason than because it is not Judaism" (see Lord:25-28). The Bene Israel remained loyal to Judaism even without knowing much about mainstream Judaism or about the multiplicity of *halachic* details. Without bigotry, the Bene Israel maintained their own identity, ethnicity and growing repertoire of Jewish practices, even while becoming educated and Westernized, and being pressured to convert to Christianity.

The Bene Israel owe a great debt of gratitude to Rev. Wilson, the Christian, and his mission schools for having taught them the Hebrew language so well that it gave them access to all the Jewish holy writings and liturgies. And, the English language and secular subjects which the Bene Israel learned in Wilson's schools opened up for them not only contacts with mainstream Judaism, but with the world of knowledge as such. However, beginning from the mid-nineteenth century, most of the rural, free mission schools for non-Christians were gradually phased out. As early as 1858 some Indian college students of non-Christian communities were setting up schools of their own without any Christian content in the curriculum. But Christian missionary activity persisted in Kolaba District in spite of reduced free schooling for non-Christians. Various missions continued trying to persuade Bene Israel to convert to Christianity but with almost no success.

There is no doubt that the mission schools in Kolaba District certainly did create a thirst for further education during the second half of the nineteenth century. Bene Israel village families, except those from the most isolated villages, were sending at least one of their children to the nearest school, and from there to a higher school in Bombay. This accelerated the pattern of migration to Bombay already begun in the eighteenth century. The nineteenth century young Bene Israel student coming from his village now had the added facility of having relatives already established in Bombay with whom he or she could live while attending school and college in Bombay. It took until 1875 for the dream of H.S. Kehimkar to become a reality, i.e. the founding of the Israelite School in Bombay, established, administered and staffed by and for the Bene Israel community. In spite of many obstacles, the school managed to secure sufficient funds and also a government grant which enabled poor Bene Israel children (of whom there were very many in the nineteenth century) to continue their education beyond primary school, when otherwise they would have become drop-outs, doomed to child labor. The Israelite School had high standards. Its curriculum included instruction in Hebrew and Jewish studies; and the school was closed on Saturdays and Jewish holidays.

At a time when Christian missionary activity among the Bene Israel in Kolaba District was at its height, Jewish teachers of Orthodox Judaism were devoting their lives to adding new dimensions, by teaching and example, to the ways of Bene Israel Jewish life. Like the Christian missionaries, the Jewish teachers also realized that at that period the Bene Israel "heartland" was by no means peripheral to the cause of Bene Israel enlightenment. So, the Jewish teachers also worked in Kolaba District. Most of these teachers were the so-called Cochin Jews.

Thekkumbhagam Synagogue, Ernakulam, Kerala.

All photographs in the book are by Ellen S. Goldberg.

Malida ceremony honoring Elijah the Prophet at Khandala, Maharashtra, site of Elijah's purported visit to India.

Meir Simon before the Holy Ark of the North Parur Synagogue, Kerala.

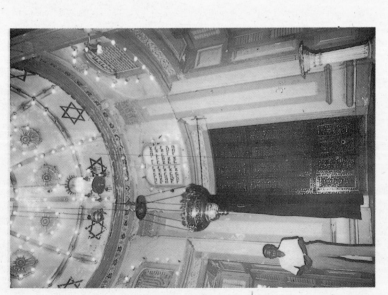

Interior of Maghen David Synagogue, Bombay.

D. M. Benjamin Rohekar, proprietor of a small Judaica shop in Bombay.

Torah processions (*haqafot*) around the Cochin Synagogue during the Mincha (afternoon) service of Simchat Torah.

Dargah (tomb) of Cochin's most eminent mystic, the seventeenth-century Qabbalist, Nehemia Mota.

Ohel David Synagogue, commonly known as Lal Deval or "Red Temple," Pune.

Miriam Ashkenazi (left) boards train for Bombay, the first leg of her emigration from Cochin to Israel. Queenie Hallegua stands in foreground.

Torah scrolls in the Holy Ark of the Cochin Synagogue.

Interior of the Cochin-style synagogue at Moshav Nevatim, Israel.

Reema Salem of Cochin inspects the wheat to be used for *matsah* (unleavened bread) for Passover.

In the eighteenth century the Bene Israel had had infrequent contacts with Cochin Jews and occasionally sought guidance from them on Jewish religious matters. Although in 1797 Samaji Hassaji Divekar died in Cochin where he had gone to obtain a Torah Scroll for the first Bene Israel synagogue, the Cochin Jews, for some unknown reason, did not send a Torah Scroll to the Bene Israel synagogue; and it was not until 1826 that a group of Jewish teachers, who belonged to the Paradesi "White" Cochin Jewish community, came to the Konkan, followed by a second group of Cochin Jewish teachers in 1833. They taught, preached, and interpreted the Bible and Jewish law to Bene Israel, not only in Bombay but also in Kolaba District, especially at Revdanda, Alibag, Ashtami, and Pali where relatively large numbers of Bene Israel lived. On weekdays the teachers from Cochin taught Jewish religion and Hebrew reading and writing to Bene Israel children. On Saturdays they conducted morning prayer services and spent Saturday afternoons with Bene Israel adults, discussing Jewish laws, customs· and beliefs. (Presumably the services of these teachers were free, perhaps in return for room and board or for very meagre wages.) One of them, Judah Ashkenazy, wrote and published for the Bene Israel a calendar of Jewish Holidays, in Marathi; it proved to be very helpful. In respect of the law forbidding work on the Sabbath, the rural Bene Israel were more observant than were many Bene Israel in Bombay Government civil service jobs, or very poor Bene Israel manual laborers in Bombay or in the small towns.

In 1838 Shelomo Salem Shurrabi, coming by boat from Cochin (although his ancestors were from Yemen), was shipwrecked off the coast of Alibag. He was rescued and nursed back to health by a Bene Israel from Alibag. Thereafter, for the rest of his life, Shurrabi became one of the most effective and beloved of the teachers of Judaism. Though he was based mainly at the second Bene Israel synagogue, which was founded in Bombay by Shurrabi in 1840-41, in Kolaba District it was also Shurrabi who was responsible for founding a synagogue in Revdanda (1842), in Alibag (1848), and in Panvel (1849).

In Kolaba District additional synagogues were built at Tale-Ghosale (1849), Pen (1863), Poynad (1866), Borlai (1869), Ambedpur (1874), Ashtami (1882), Mhsala (1886), Post Chorde (1892), and Nandgaon (1896). Note, however, that no new synagogues were established in Kolaba District in the twentieth century, although in the twentieth century a few of the above were rebuilt: Alibag Synagogue (1910), Mhsala (1921), Poynad (1933), and Nandgaon (1945). S.J. Kolabkar's booklet, *Kolaba Travels Investigations*, printed in Karachi in 1946, mentions three more synagogues in Kolaba District, namely at Ghosale-Virjoli, Murud, and Shriwardhan, but the booklet does not mention when they were founded. Synagogues were built in villages where relatively large numbers of Bene Israel families were living. Each synagogue also served the Bene Israel who lived in the surrounding villages, some of which were not even within easy commuting distance; or were not accessible during monsoon flooding; or, if near the coast, were separated by backwaters which could be crossed on foot only during low tide.

The Jewish teachers introduced the Bene Israel of Kolaba District to synagogue-centered communal organization. Even before a synagogue would be built, the congregation (sometimes just barely a *minyan*[18]) would meet in each other's homes. The leader (*Mukkadam*) of the congregation was often the same person who was already headman of the Bene Israel families in a given village. He was assisted by four or five local Bene Israel elderly councillors (*Choglas*). And there was a local Bene Israel treasurer (*Gabbai*), and a local Bene Israel Shamash (sexton and herald for the congregation). The *Hazan* (cantor or reader of the synagogue liturgy) was until the twentieth century either a Cochini, a Baghdadi, or a Yemenite Jew "imported" from Bombay by a particular Kolaba District congregation. The *Hazan* usually also performed the duties of *Shochet* (ritual slaughterer of fowl or goats,

---

[18]*Minyan* (Hebrew): Ten Jewish males (thirteen years of age or older), being the minimum number of persons required for conducting Jewish congregational prayer. (In Reform and Conservative Judaism today, women are also considered eligible for a *minyan*.)

never cattle, for *Kosher* meat), *Mohel* (ritual circumsizer), and *Sopher* (Hebrew scribe and teacher). Unlike most Bene Israel, their Kazis had not changed with the times, nor had they widened their knowledge, Jewish or secular. So, they had gradually lost the respect and honor formerly paid to them by all Bene Israel. Some Kazis were still officiating as late as 1885, but mainly in villages which had no synagogues. The *Jamat* (general assembly) consisted of all the adult males of the congregation. Each Kolaba District synagogue was independent, with no central coordination. No congregation had the equivalent of an ordained rabbi. The congregation as a whole owned the synagogue building and the land on which it stood, which sometimes was extensive enough to be rented out to tenant farmers, the income going into the synagogue treasury to maintain the premises, dispense charity, purchase utensils, mats, etc., for use at communal, as well as private, Bene Israel functions and feasts. Next to each synagogue was a small building housing a regulation-size pool for ritual immersion and bath (*mikvah*). The more affluent Bene Israel made donations in cash or in kind. Synagogue income also accrued from the custom of bidding for the privilege of reading from the Torah and of reciting blessings accompanying each reading. For the Bene Israel, whether in an urban or in a rural area, the synagogue became not only their religious center; it was also the focal point of their social and community life. Some villages without a synagogue but with more than a handful of Bene Israel families might have had their own Bene Israel burial ground (as did villages with a synagogue). But the problem of burial in isolated villages, with only two or three Bene Israel families and with no other alternative, was solved by interment in the local Muslim cemetery. Relations between Bene Israel and their Muslim and Hindu neighbors were friendly, and each respected the religious practices of the other.[19] There simply was no "anti-Semitic" hostility. Early writers, foreign to the area, either overlooked the

---

[19]In Kolaba District there has been an absence of Hindu-Muslim violence such as has flared up from time to time in northern India and recently also in Bombay.

Bene Israel completely or assumed that they were Muslims. Even in Kolaba District the percentage of Bene Israel compared with that of other religions, ethnic groups, sub-castes, etc., was so minute that in some Kolaba District villages where no Bene Israel were living, the population probably never knew that Bene Israel existed.

Although the Bene Israel in Kolaba District during the 1830s and 1840s had been taught by strictly orthodox teachers how to follow the rules of *Halacha* in minute detail, it was not long before they veered toward less strict observance, due partly to practical considerations[20] and very likely also in reaction to the conflicting influences of secular education, elements of Christianity, Western enlightenment, and Jewish Orthodoxy. The Bene Israel were being confronted for the first time by all four pressures virtually simultaneously. The result was that the Bene Israel, even in the nineteenth century, were in some respects closer to modern Conservative Judaism than to Orthodoxy. In Kolaba District this process had evolved entirely on its own and within the context of its rural life-style. It retained some unique elements of what I would call "Bene Israel *Halacha* of the *Kazi* era", especially in the observance of certain Jewish holidays. The entire spectrum, i.e. *Kazi*-era Jewish observances, mainstream Jewish observances, and a mix of the two were being practised contemporaneously by Bene Israel in Kolaba District during the latter half of the nineteenth century and even until beyond the first half of the twentieth century. The preference for one alternative above another depended upon such variables as a given Bene Israel family's finances, isolation, distance from a synagogue, and firsthand familiarity with practitioners of mainstream Jewish customs.

---

[20]Practical considerations such as: a) Limitations of poverty—not being able to afford three sets of utensils connected with food for dairy, meat and Passover meals; no bicycle or bullock cart to travel to too distant a synagogue; not being able to afford the loss of a single day's pay (if employed by others) and therefore working on Sabbath and Jewish holidays. b) Government employ required working on Saturdays and often necessitated riding to work also on Saturdays.

A Zionist Association had been founded in Bombay by Baghdadi Jews in 1920, but the Bene Israel did not begin joining the association unil 1940. Its offices were located in Bombay and most of their activities centered in and around the city, affecting the villages only in respect of efforts to attract the Bene Israel village youths. India became an independent country on August 15, 1947. Israel became independent on May 14, 1948. Large scale immigration to Israel by Indian Jews began in 1949 (see Isenberg:268-273 and 302-303). In the beginning most of the adult Bene Israel emigrés had lived and worked in Bombay. Their emigration from India was motivated by a complex of religious, economic and idealistic factors. Bene Israel youth were often the first to leave India for Israel, to be joined later by their parents and grandparents. Before leaving India, many of them spent some time learning basic Hebrew and were given some agricultural training. Bene Israel boys and girls, mostly teenagers, came not only from Bombay and other cities but also from the villages of Kolaba District. The Jewish Agency arranged for the village youngsters, while in Bombay, to stay in dormitories set up on synagogue properties or on the Kadoorie (formerly called The Israelite) School premises. Large scale emigration of adults from Kolaba District did not take place until 1968-1973, drastically— often completely—depleting the Bene Israel population of Kolaba District villages.

Almost all Bene Israel who had emigrated to Israel before 1968 preferred to settle in Israeli cities. Only a handful of Bene Israel settled permamently in an agricultural village or in a kibbutz (rural collective settlement). When the adult Bene Israel villagers finally came to Israel, the desire to live close to their respective urbanized relatives who had preceded them was more important to them than to continue living in rural surroundings. So they too settled in Israeli cities or in the large new "development" towns, living in multi-family apartment buildings. Thus ended the centuries-long saga of Bene Israel living in rural villages.

In India the Bene Israel population had grown from about 8,000 in 1836 to a peak of about 25,000 in 1951. The number of Bene Israel and their offspring living in Israel today approaches

45,000. I have no idea how many former Kolaba District Bene Israel villagers are alive today in Israel, nor in the other countries of the Bene Israel Diaspora. But of one thing I am sure: with every passing year there are fewer and fewer Bene Israel former villagers who are still alive and available to tell us about their own lives and what they can remember about generations past.

What follows are excerpts culled from life stories of some Bene Israel who were born and lived as villagers in Kolaba District. These vignettes personalize many particulars already indicated above but which, up to this point, have been only in the form of generalizations.

Gerry Zalizar's account of his visit with Bene Israel residents of the Kolaba District of Wakrul provides interesting details. The route from Bombay to Wakrul (about ninety miles) required going through hilly, panther-infested jungle before reaching the village. Three Bene Israel families, a total of twenty-five persons, lived in Wakrul at that time in three thatch-roofed, two-room houses situated side by side. Zalizar sat on the verandah of the house of the "leader" of the three families, together with all their menfolk. The "leader" wore the white Nehru-Congress cap which was then popular throughout India, and all the others wore caps which had been embroidered by the women of the family. The "leader" was also the employer of the men of Wakrul who felled trees. He arranged to have the trees cut into size for firewood which he sold in nearby towns. Only the three household heads and Zalizar did the talking (through an interpreter). The house had no running water, no toilets, no electricity, no windows. There was only one kerosene lamp in the entire village. Above the entrance to the house, near the *mezuzah*,[21] hung a paper on which there was a brown impression of a child's hand. It was brown from the now

---

[21]*Mezuzah* (Hebrew): Literal meaning "doorpost." Also the name of a small closed receptacle (usually artistically wrought) containing a small piece of parchment on which, in tiny Hebrew lettering, are written the verses of the *Shema*: from Deuteronomy 6:4-9 and 5:13-21, and from Numbers 15:37-41. Jews are supposed to affix a *Mezuzah* on the doorposts to rooms in their houses and other buildings, and on their gates.

discolored blood of the "paschal lamb"—actually of a goat—in which the hand was dipped just before the previous Passover, and left there to bring good luck and to ward off evil. Each of the three families had had eight or nine children and in each family two or three children had already died of malaria or typhus. The nearest doctor was a Jewish (Bene Israel) woman who lived in the town of Pen, which was impossible to reach during the monsoon season. Only the eldest man among them had ever travelled to Bombay or had seen the sea coast. The grandfather of this old man had left Wakrul forty years ago to live in Bombay where he had set up a business selling firewood. Neither he nor any of the other relatives in Bombay ever came to visit the relatives who still remained in Wakrul. Wakrul's three Bene Israel families always had very good relations with Wakrul's non-Jewish residents. The men on the verandah asked Zalizar if it was true that in America there are buildings fifty stories high and that you get up to the fiftieth floor "in a machine driven by hand". For the Jewish holidays all three Bene Israel families would go to the town of Pen where a synagogue was built "about fifty years ago", they said, and where Bene Israel would gather, having come from twenty or twenty-five surrounding villages. A *Hazan* would come from Bombay to officiate for the holidays. These villagers didn't know Hebrew but they knew when to say "amen" while in synagogue. Kosher meat was brought to Wakrul from Pen except during the monsoon when the roads were flooded; so, during the monsoon all of Wakrul's Bene Israel were strictly vegetarian. When a male child was born, a qualified Mohel was informed and would come from Bombay to perform the circumcision. If the birth occurred during monsoon, the ceremony would have to be postponed until better weather would make access to the village possible.

One wishes that Zalizar had found out many more details. Zalizar's visit to Wakrul took place not in the nineteenth century, but in 1962![22]

[22]Zalizar, Gerry, "The Road to Wakrul," a Hebrew article ("Ha-Derech l'Wakrul") published in *Gesher Quarterly*, ninth year, 35/2, 1963, pp. 118-121, published by the Israel Branch of the World Jewish Congress.

Dadaji and his Village

From my own lengthy sessions[23] with some former Bene Israel villagers, my favorite life history is that of a tall, erect man speaking with great assurance in his mother tongue, Marathi. I'll call him Dadaji. He was born in 1901 in the village of Parali, very near the eastern border of Kolaba District. His family had lived in Parali for seven generations, which would go back to the mid-eighteenth century. Yet his surname was not Paralkar or Paralikar (I know of no Bene Israel surname related to Parali). Rather, his surname related to a village more than 50 miles to the southwest of Parali, about 20 miles from the sea coast. The 1961 Government of India Census Survey of Parali states that as of 1961, Sudhagad *tehsil* (sub division) of Kolaba District (in which *tehsil* Parali is located) had a larger Jewish (i.e. Bene Israel) population than did any of the other twelve *tehsils* of Kolaba District. The total population of Parali was 730. It lies on a north-south State Highway, but had no direct route connecting it to Pen, the nearest town which is thirty-five miles to the west. The nearest bus stop was five-eighths of a mile eastward. The nearest telegraph office (in which there was the nearest telephone) was in the village of Pali, twelve miles away. Parali did have a primary school, while Pali was near a secondary school. The nearest post office, as well as a modern medical dispensary, were more than a mile and a quarter away. Parali did not yet have electricity. All water had to be drawn either from the river, wells or ponds. Rice, the staple crop, was dependent upon heavy monsoon rains (June to September). Parali had eleven rice mills and one oil press. There was a weekly open market on Saturdays.

Dadaji told me there were 150 families living in Parali: twenty-five of them were Bene Israel (of which twenty owned their own land); ten were Muslim families; and all the rest, or about seventy-five per cent of Parali's population, were Hindu. Dadaji

---

[23]I call them sessions, not interviews, because I deliberately asked very few questions and did very little talking. What I did request was the respondent's life history—a flow of memories—and whatever he or she could tell me concerning earlier generations of Bene Israel.

had married when he was twenty-five years old and his bride, who came from another village, was fifteen. Neither of them had ever gone to school, nor could they read or write. Dadaji's family homestead usually had about thirteen persons of the extended family all living together: Dadaji, his wife, their daughter (who was their only child), Dadaji's two brothers and their respective wives and children, and Dadaji's three unmarried sisters. The joint family owned not only the house, but the ten acres of land on which it stood. The house originally consisted of one front room and a kitchen. Each subsequent generation kept repairing and adding to it, providing each married couple with a separate room.

In Dadaji's day there was also a storeroom for storing food to be consumed between harvests; a small room to keep about ten chickens for their eggs and some for eating. Entirely separate was a shed in which they kept their fifteen water buffaloes, a pair of bullocks and a few cows. The family oil press was attached to this shed. It was the only oil mill in Parali, and Dadaji was in charge of it. The grindstone was propelled by a blindfolded bullock harnessed to the apparatus, which went round and round. Dadaji processed sesame and mustard seeds, coconuts and peanuts, all grown on his land, as well as seeds, etc., which were brought to him for grinding by other villagers who paid him for his services either in kind or cash. He processed edible as well as inedible (for lamplighting) oils. However, after modern oil mills began producing oil, the competition from them rendered traditional processing no longer profitable.

As his ancestors had done before him, Dadaji used much of the family land to grow rice, which required certain strenuous seasonal work done by everyone in the family working together with twenty-five seasonal laborers. The hired people were mostly Muslims, but there were some Hindus too. They received daily wages and food for their services. At these times Dadaji's wife cooked for all the hired help, as well as for all members of the joint family. The straw left over from the rice harvest was used to feed the family's cows, bullocks and buffaloes. A whole year's supply of rice was kept for family use. Then Dadaji himself would take his bullock cart and pile onto it the family's surplus produce of rice and oils, and also other wares such as charcoal and fish nets produced by other Parali villagers. All this Dadaji peddled throughout the surrounding villages. Since the family produced practically all their own food—except for salt, sugar, tea and their favorite kind of powdered chili—they had little need for cash.

Most of Parali's population were Hindus, and Dadaji enjoyed participating in some of the Hindu celebrations, particularly a certain Hindu festival when the horns of all bullocks were painted and decorated with garlands and small bells, and were then paraded around the village. It was a way of showing appreciation for one's beasts of burden. Dadaji would even donate some cash for the closing function of the day which, however, he chose not to attend because it included a feast[24] and a Hindu religious ceremony. Dadaji explained: "They are my neighbors and good friends and I like to help them. But their religion is not my religion."

In Parali there was neither a synagogue nor a prayer hall. Dadaji and family observed the Sabbath as follows: Food was prepared on Friday and kept warm on a low grid placed over an ample supply of dried cattle dung patties which were ignited before sundown and which burn very slowly, with no odor. Every Friday promptly at 4 p.m. all work outside and inside the house ceased. The Sabbath lamp, suspended on the wall in the front room, was lit before sunset by Dadaji's wife who recited the appropriate blessing. Before the evening meal Dadaji recited *Kiddush*[25] over the local type of bread and a glass of grape or raisin juice. The nearest synagogue was too far away to attend services there. For the three-week period—which included the Jewish holidays of Rosh Hashanah (New Year), Yom Kippur (Day of Atonement), and the eight days of Succoth (Festival of Tabernacles), ending with Simchat Torah (Rejoicing in the Torah)—prayer services were held in Parali, at one Bene Israel house

---

[24]Many non-Brahmin Hindus are not vegetarians and therefore the meal probably would not have been kosher (i.e. according to Jewish dietary laws).

[25]*Kiddush*: Hebrew prayer sanctifying the Sabbath or a Jewish holiday, accompanied by a blessing over wine.

or another, sometimes with a *Hazan* hired from elsewhere, or with a Bene Israel resident of Parali who knew how to lead the prayers. About once a year Dadaji would take his wife and daughter to Bombay, a four-hour journey. In Bombay they would stay at the home of relatives. Dadaji made a point of attending synagogue on Sabbath or a Jewish holiday whenever he was in Bombay. He never learned to read Hebrew, nor had he learned by heart large parts of the liturgy. Passover was always spent at home in Parali, with a total ban on eating any food which the family had not themselves harvested and processed. During Passover they used no sugar because it had not been prepared by Jews. Instead of tea, they brewed certain leaves they grew on their property. Dried spices were taboo because they had been dried long before Passover. Their unleavened bread (*matzah*) was made from a dough of rice flour baked immediately so that no natural leavening had time to take place.

Dadaji's daughter finished Seventh Standard at Parali Primary School. Like her mother she married young. After marriage she and her husband went to live in Bombay where she continued her schooling through the Tenth Standard. She actually had filled out an application to attend a teacher-training course in Bombay, but she became pregnant and embarked upon motherhood instead. She and her husband had three children in Bombay before they emigrated to Israel. A few years later, in 1968, after enjoying one week in Bombay, Dadaji and his wife also left for Israel. They settled in the city of Beer Sheva in a small walk-up apartment close to where their daughter and her family live. Dadaji worked as a gardener for the municipality of Beer Sheva until he was seventy-four years old, when he retired. In 1978 he told me that only one Bene Israel family was still living in Parali.

Village Life, followed by Four Years in Bombay: Segulla

Segulla was born in a village about midway down Kolaba District's sea coast, in Murud Tehsil, very near its border with

Alibag *tehsil*. (Alibag *tehsil* has the largest number of Bene Israel surname-linked villages.) There were three Bene Israel families living in her village, no Muslims, and about 300 Hindu families. Segulla and her family had very close Hindu friends. Her father had inherited his land and house from his father. It was a large, one-storeyed house with a thatched roof under which they dried vegetables and spices for use by the family during the rainy season; here too they stored extra jars and jugs of homemade pickles and chutneys. Segulla's father had gone to school through the Fourth Standard (taught in the Marathi medium) and Segulla attended the same primary school. Her mother was able to read and write in Marathi but had had no other schooling. Segulla's paternal grandfather had been a carpenter as well as a farmer, and he had taught carpentry and house building to Segulla's father, using traditional tools. Her father spent much time working on the family land together with Segulla's three brothers, with additional help being hired only seasonally. The family made some oil from their own sesame seeds, but only enough for the family's needs. One of the other Bene Israel families in the village processed oil especially for sale to others. Segulla's family owned one bullock and cart, four or five cows, and a few chickens (for their eggs). Chicken was eaten only on special occasions such as on Jewish and Hindu holidays. There were several Hindu customs which, over the generations, Segulla's family had adopted, but nothing that was basically incompatible with the Jewish religion.

Sometimes on Jewish holidays the whole family would walk the few miles to a nearby village where there was a synagogue, but for Yom Kippur the entire family always remained at home. Segulla was sentimental about the way her family used to observe Yom Kippur which had deeply impressed her. She described the atmosphere of their home on Yom Kippur as being "very like a synagogue". All windows and doors were closed. Everything indoors was covered with white cloths and all members of the family (there were no guests on Yom Kippur) were dressed in white. A few hours before sunset of Yom Kippur eve (as was their wont every Friday before the Sabbath began), everyone would bathe by first anointing the entire body with homemade coconut oil, then removing the oil with a certain kind of flour, and finally rinsing with fresh water. They ate and drank nothing from before sundown on Yom Kippur eve until after dark on Yom Kippur, and after having recited outdoors the benediction for the new moon.[26] They spoke very little to each other during the entire twenty-six hours and were careful neither to utter nor to hear anything bad. When anyone in the family could read Hebrew or knew Hebrew prayers by heart, they would recite them. No one in the family did any work whatsoever during Yom Kippur. Segulla said, "On Yom Kippur we did not even milk our cows. Our Hindu neighbors quietly took care of that for us. They respected our Yom Kippur custom and would say, 'Today the Bene Israel will not talk'. While our family was outside blessing the moon, the neighbors would unobtrusively enter our courtyard, leave the milk which they had collected for us from our cows, and silently go away."

Every year just before the Jewish New Year, and again before Passover, the exterior and interior walls of the whole house were whitewashed. After the whitewashing for Passover the imprint of a hand dipped in the blood of a goat was pressed onto the outside wall at the entrance to the house; and this was never covered over by the next whitewashing which took place just before Rosh Hashanah. The imprint remained intact until the next Passover when the old imprint was finally covered with fresh whitewash and another imprint made. For each Passover everything in the house was thoroughly cleaned, and the insides of all brass cooking vessels were re-lined and thus made new for Passover each year. Whatever clay vessels were to be used were purchased anew for each Passover.

When Segulla was twelve years old her father obtained a

[26]Even though Yom Kippur falls ten days after the Jewish New Year (which coincides with the first day of the Jewish lunar month, Tishri), the sage Maimonides had fixed anywhere between the first to the sixteenth of the month as appropriate for reciting the blessing for a new moon. This blessing is recited only if and when the new moon is visible, and preferably immediately following the Saturday night prayer service.

construction job with a foreign company in Bombay. He took his wife and children to live with him in a rented flat in Bombay, and the children attended Bombay schools. In his job Segulla's father learned many new techniques and became familiar with modern tools and machines. Also while they lived in Bombay, her father studied and learned Hebrew. But after four years, the foreign firm which had employed him closed down. During these four years the family had always returned to their village home to spend their vacations there. However, after those four years they returned to live once again in their native village.

Segulla married a man from a different village situated not on the coast but inland, nineteen miles away. Her husband's surname bore the same name as his village of residence. While Segulla lived there, there were eleven other Bene Israel joint families living in the same village. And there were also several Muslim families. There was one separate quarter where all the Muslims lived, and another separate quarter for all the Brahmins of the village. Hindus of lower castes, engaged in various occupations, lived in separate neighborhoods of their own. However, there was no separate quarter for the Bene Israel families. Some of them lived in the Muslim quarter, and some among various Hindu groups; but no Bene Israel family lived in the Brahmin quarter. Segulla and her husband lived only a short time with his family in his village and then, in 1969, the young couple emigrated to Israel. As for Segulla's native village, her parents were the very last of its three Bene Israel families to leave for Israel, where they joined Segulla and her growing family.

Dinah, Fluent in English

Dinah's native village was located inland and her father's surname was linked to this village. Her father was a carpenter and also specialized in growing on his own land a large variety of green vegetables which he sold locally. Their village had a one storey thatch-roofed synagogue which attracted Bene Israel of many other villages from miles around, coming on foot, or on bicycle, bullock cart or by train, and then walking a few more miles. The "out-of-towners" would usually arrive at Dinah's village before sundown on the eve of a Jewish holiday or Sabbath. They would spend one or two nights in the home of one or another Bene Israel family of that village, in order to be able to attend both the evening and the morning synagogue services. The house of Dinah's joint family was big enough to give overnight accommodation to as many as fifty guests, provided that each guest brought his or her own bedroll or mat on which to sleep on the floor. (Fortunately, many Indian joint families are well equipped for and accustomed to cooking for a large number of guests who, more often than not, are relatives.)

Dinah completed elementary school in her own village, which also has a high school and, like its elementary school, was taught in the Marathi medium. But Dinah's parents, who did not themselves know much English, wanted their children to learn English well. Therefore Dinah, her sister and brother, as each came of high school age, were sent to English-medium high schools in Bombay. The girls attended a good convent school. Their brother completed his studies at the ORT[27] Manual Training School in Bombay, after which he found a job in Bombay as a mechanic, where he worked for two years until he left for Israel. Dinah and her sister emigrated to Israel with a Youth Aliyah (immigration to Israel) group. Eventually their parents came to live in Israel too.

Conclusions

Nowadays, the history of Bene Israel existence in Kolaba District lives only in the memory of today's older generation, those born in Kolaba District and who lived there as villagers. In the course of three centuries, three differing identities—sometimes overlapping—have characterized the lifestyles of India's Bene Israel villagers:

[27]ORT: Organization for Rehabilitation through Training, with branches and schools worldwide.of the World Jewish Congress.

1) As long as they remained in their villages, their lifestyle (apart only from the super-position of their specific Jewish customs) remained typical of the then-prevailing Indian lifestyle of the general rural population of Kolaba District.

2) As opportunities for education and then for higher education and for new kinds of employment beckoned under British rule, more and more of the Bene Israel left their villages and gradually exchanged their rural identity for a new, urban identity.

3) Notwithstanding the trend noted above, the Bene Israel villagers and erstwhile villagers have held on fast to their Jewish identity. Also they have continued to come closer to mainstream Judaism. Ultimately, the majority of Bene Israel emigrated from India to Israel.

Even though there were, and continue to be, notable instances of Bene Israel fissiparousness, Bene Israel community life as such—which hardly existed among them in the eighteenth century—became an anchor of Bene Israel identification in the nineteenth century and continues to be so today. The Bene Israel now in Israel and in other lands, as well as the 5,000 or so Bene Israel remaining in India, do not identify with their rural roots. With no more visits to the family and homestead in the village, all links to rural identity have been severed. With very few exceptions, all Bene Israel are now city dwellers, living in nuclear family units, no longer as joint families. With varying degrees of education and with a strong sense of Bene Israel community, today's typical Bene Israel is affiliated to a Bene Israel synagogue or to one or more Bene Israel or other Jewish organizations.

Concerning Bene Israel identity as Indians, the following generalizations suggest themselves: The Bene Israel who remain in India are full-fledged citizens of India in name, in deed, and in self-perception. For the Bene Israel who have emigrated from India, their Indianness is a matter of nostalgic affection for and appreciation of India, but without regret for having chosen a different national identity. Their children lack the nostalgia, and some of them evince no curiosity to learn about India. On the other hand, many of them look forward to visits to India as being important to them in terms of their own roots.

Sources cited

Cadell, Sir Patrick. 1938. *History of the Bombay Army.* Bombay: Longmans Green and Company.

Census Reports of 1961 on *Village Surveys in Maharasthra,* inclusive of *The Kolaba District Census Handbook for 1961,* Bombay, Director of Government Printing and Stationery, Maharashtra State, 1964.

Isenberg, Shirley Berry. 1988. *India's Bene Israel: A Comprehensive Inquiry and Sourcebook.* Berkeley: Judah L. Magnes Museum and Bombay: Popular Prakashan.

Israel, Benjamin Jacob. 1984. *The Bene Israel of India: Some Studies.* Bombay: Orient Longmans.

Kehimkar, Haeem Samuel. 1937. *The History of the Bene-Israel of India.* Ed. Immanuel Olsvanger. Tel Aviv: Dayag Press. [written in 1897.]

Lord, Rev J. Henry. 1894. *The Jewsih Mission Field in the Bombay Diocese.* Byculla, Bombay: Education Society's Steam Press. (Paper read before the Bombay Diocesan Conference, March 1883.)

Smith, George. 1878. *Life of John Wilson, D.D., F.R.S., for Fifty Years Philanthropist and Scholar in the East.* London: John Murray.

Wilson, Rev John. 1840. "Abstract of an Account of the Beni-Israel of Bombay,"(read before the Bombay Branch of the Royal Asiatic Society at the Anniversary Meeting in November 1838 and 1839), Bombay, *The Oriental Christian Spectator* 11/1 (January):27-36.

Zalizar, Gerry. 1963. "Ha-Derech l'Wakrul," ("The Road to Wakrul") *Gesher Quarterly* 35/2:118-121; in Hebrew; published by the Israel Branch of the World Jewish Congress.

4

Indian-Jewish Identity of the Bene Israel during the British Raj[1]

Joan G. Ròland

"Microscopic" has been the term most frequently used to describe the Jewish communities in India, for at their peak in the early 1950s, the total Jewish population never exceeded thirty thousand in a country which at the time had over three hundred million people. Now, there are barely five thousand Jews left out of a total Indian population of approximately nine hundred million. And yet, what is remarkable is that India is perhaps the one country in the world where Jews have never been exposed to anti-Semitism or religious persecution at the hands of their hosts, while continuously maintaining their identity. Although the question of identity among the Cochin and Baghdadi Jews is also a fascinating subject, this paper focuses on the Bene Israel, the largest of the Jewish communities, which numbered perhaps 20,000 at its peak.

A lack of reliable evidence prevents us from determining the actual origin of the Bene Israel and the exact time that the group appeared in western India. Bene Israel traditions maintain that they are descendants of one of the Ten Tribes of Israel.[2] According to their legends, the ancestors of the Bene Israel left northern Israel around 175 B.C.E., or perhaps later, and were shipwrecked near the

[1]The University Press of New England has kindly granted permission to reproduce in her chapter in the present work material that appeared in slightly different form in the introduction, chapter one and the conclusion of Professor Roland's book, *Jews in British India: Identity in a Colonial Era* (Hanover, NH, 1989).

[2]Strizower (1971:10-15) suggests that the Ten Tribes theory of origin may have originated with Christian missionaries or Jewish travellers, and then passed into Bene Israel tradition.

village of Navgaon on the Konkan Coast of western India, twenty-
six miles south of Bombay. Only seven men and seven women were
said to have survived.[3] Scholars have proposed different theories of
place and date of origin of this community: that they arrived during
the reign of King Solomon in the tenth century B.C.E., before the
ten tribes separated from the other two (Israel 1982:19); during the
mid-eighth century B.C.E., before the fall of Samaria, the capital of
the Kingdom of Israel (Samuel 1963); that they came from Yemen
in the middle of the first millennium C.E. (Wilson 1865, cited by
Strizower 1971:19, n. 11)[4]; or that they were part of the dispersal
that took place after the destruction of the Second Temple in 70 C.E.
There may have been more than one immigration. A knowledgeable Bene Israel favors a theory that the Bene Israel came to India
in the fifth or sixth century C.E. from either southern Arabia or
Persia. (see Israel 1982:20; Godbey 1930:317, 345; and Strizower
1971:15). But as there are no written records, inscriptions, or other
evidence to confirm or disprove any of these conjectures, and since
the earliest extant documentation dates only from the seventeenth
century, the origins of the Bene Israel remain shrouded in legend.

The early history of the Bene Israel is also obscure. From
Navgaon, they gradually dispersed throughout the coastal Konkan
villages, living in small communities of perhaps no more than one
hundred people. Intermarriage with native women probably
occurred to some extent. Cut off for centuries from contact with the
mainstream of Jewish life, the Bene Israel gradually forgot all but
a few essential elements of the Jewish religion. They continued to
observe dietary laws and circumcision and abstained from work on
the Sabbath. They celebrated the festivals of the New Year, Day of
Atonement, Passover, Purim and Feast of Ingathering, reciting the
Shema, the most important prayer of the Jews, on these and other

[3]Hayeem Kehimkar, the classic historian of his community, believed that the
Jews arrived around 175 B.C.E. (Kehimkar 1937: 6-12, 15). The shipwreck legend
is similar to that of the Chitpavan Brahmins of Maharashtra.

[4]Wilson, a prominent missionary who worked with the Bene Israel in the mid-
nineteenth century, had revised his original theory that the Bene Israel were
descendants of the Ten Tribes who had settled in India at an earlier date (Wilson
1847:667-79).

important occasions. Given their long isolation, the maintenance of these traditions seems remarkable. For the rest, they slowly assimilated into their surroundings. Having no Hebrew prayer books, Bible, or Talmud, they forgot most of their Hebrew language and prayers (Israel 1963:6). They adopted the regional dress as well as the local language, Marathi, as their mother tongue. Even their names began to show signs of assimilation. First names were Indianized: Samuel became Samaji; Ezekiel, Hassaji; Isaac, Issaji. They developed traditional Marathi surnames by adding *kar* (inhabitant of) to the names of the villages where they originally resided. Nowadays, the Bene Israel have reverted to traditional biblical first names and also biblical surnames, often patronyms (Weil 1977:201-219 and Israel 1984:120-166).

The Bene Israel also adopted certain social customs from their Hindu and Muslim neighbors, such as laws of inheritance, ceremonial food offerings, and observance of certain marriage and funeral customs, but these did not affect Jewish ritual (Israel 1963:6). They engaged in agriculture and oil-pressing, gradually becoming known as *Shanwar telis* (Saturday oilmen), since they would not work on the Sabbath. This castelike designation placed them at the lower end of the Konkan class structure, since farming and oil-pressing were not particularly prestigious occupations.[5]

Many Bene Israel date an early revival of their Jewish heritage to somewhere between the eleventh and the fifteenth centuries C.E., when a David Rahabi recognized them as Jews and began to teach them the Hebrew language, as well as the liturgy, scriptures, rituals, and ceremonies of Judaism that they had forgotten. Most likely, this David Rahabi was actually a mid-eighteenth century Cochini Jew who, while serving as an agent of the Dutch East India Company, encountered the Bene Israel in Bombay, recognized them as Jews from their practices and, through his teaching, brought them into the

---

[5] By the mid-eighteenth century, oil-pressing was no longer the prominent occupation of the Bene Israel, but they still retained the name. For a discussion of how the Bene Israel fit into the caste system and their own assimilation of some of the values, see Strizower 1971:21-31.

mainstream of Judaism.[6]

By the middle of the eighteenth century, the Bene Israel population of the Konkan probably did not exceed five thousand. At this time, they began moving from the villages to the towns and then to Bombay, which was developing under the British and needed skilled tradesmen and artisans of all kinds. Bombay offered educational opportunities as well as employment, and the British East India Company was still seeking to expand its native regiments there.[7] The first Bene Israel synagogue was completed in Bombay in 1796.[8] By 1833, one-third of the total number of Bene Israel lived in Bombay. They enlisted in the regiments, took up skilled trades, became clerks in government service and with private firms, and eventually also found work in the mills of the Sassoons, the Iraqi Jews (Roth 1941:58).

A second religious renaissance began in the first decade of the nineteenth century. In 1826 and again in 1833, small groups of pious, idealistic Cochin Jews arrived in Bombay to teach the Bene Israel more Jewish ritual and ceremonials and to acquaint them with their heritage. Their efforts were augmented by those of the Arabic speaking Jews from Iraq, who were also settling in Bombay at the time.[9] A most important role in this religious revival was played by Christian missionaries who, after the ban on missionary activity in

[6]See Israel 1982: 14-20 for a full discussion of these theories. See also Kehimkar 1937: 41, 45-47, and Strizower 1971: 35-38. Although other early travelers and even Arab historians refer to Jews in India, there is no proof that these Jews are Bene Israel. See Timberg 1986:4, 10 n.3.

[7]Throughout the eighteenth century, the three European-founded ports of Calcutta, Bombay and Madras tended to be settled on a caste basis, as in other Indian cities, and much of the local government was actually in the hands of caste-based groups living in their own quarters, their *mohallas*.

[8]An oft-told legend attributes the founding of this synagogue to a Bene Israel *commandant* in the British Native Infantry Regiment, Samuel Ezekiel Divekar, who built it out of gratitude for having been released from captivity by Tippu Sultan. See Joseph 1986:361-366.

[9]The group which arrived in 1826 also included a Michael Sargon, a Cochin Jew who had converted to Christianity and was employed by the Madras Missionary Society. Sargon worked among the Bene Israel, opening six Marathi schools which lasted until 1832. Although he became quite involved in communal affairs, he did not seek to convert the Bene Israel (Fischel 1962: 140-143).

India was lifted in 1813, exerted a vital influence on the Bene Israel, particularly through their educational endeavors. The American Marathi Mission (Congregational) and the Free Church of Scotland established many schools for the Bene Israel, where they taught Hebrew (see Isenberg 1988: 65-90).

The missionaries were hopeful that the Bene Israel, already monotheists, could eventually be brought to accept Christ as the Messiah. To this end, they translated books of the so-called Old Testament into Marathi and developed Hebrew grammars in Marathi so that the community could become familar with the religion and language of its ancestors. Absorbing the Protestant emphasis on the importance of the text of the Bible, the Bene Israel became less concerned about rabbinical teaching than about the scriptures themselves. Missionaries also recorded early Bene Israel beliefs and practices as they were related to them by the community. But as responsive as the Bene Israel were to the missionaries' educational overtures, they rarely took the final step of conversion. They would reply to missionary arguments, "We do not know the replies to your questions, but our learned men elsewhere do. Ask them" (Isenberg 1988: 83 and Israel 1963:10-11).

Missionary encouragement led to a rash of publishing and translation from Hebrew into Marathi undertaken by the Bene Israel themselves in the second half of the nineteenth century. But missionary activity also stimulated the spread of English among the Bene Israel, which enabled them to become acquainted with books of Jewish interest published in England and the United States. Soon fewer translations of religious works into Marathi were necessary (Israel 1963:13). This access to English materials naturally increased the Bene Israel's sense of belonging to a larger Jewish community, gradually reducing their isolation and their dependence on other Jewish communities and missionaries in India for religious instruction and sustenance. They had been Jewish in a particularly Indian way; now they adopted the beliefs, practices and concerns of Jewish communities elsewhere.

Defining the Jews of India has its own set of special problems. There are indeed two interrelated contexts in which the position of

the Jews of India may be observed, both of which can serve as a
focus for exploring identity and social change: caste and ethnic
pluralism. Although caste was not necessarily the most significant
aspect of the Indian Jewish environment, it was certainly a unique
feature —as distinct from the experience of other Jewish communities in the world. Indeed, caste cannot be overlooked in any study
of groups in India, even if one is writing about a non-Hindu
minority. Indian civilization is also marked by a form of absorption,
of tolerance, of the acceptance of "unity in diversity". Hinduism is
prepared to affirm, in a culturally pluralistic way, the truth of all
religions (Cohn 1971:3; Srinivas 1966:14, 75). One of the ways in
which Hindu toleration of small minority communities has expressed itself has been through the almost castelike designation of
varied groups. Groups such as Christians, Jews, and Parsis in
particular were thought to have certain traditions, roles, culture—
so that a live-and-let-live policy could develop within a caste
environment (see Schermerhorn 1978).

In the eighteenth and nineteenth centuries, the Bene Israel often
refrained from widow remarriage and beef-eating—sometimes all
meat-eating. Perhaps they were attempting to raise their position
socially or to rise in public esteem by imitating the behavior of the
higher castes (a form of Sanskritization, to use M.N. Srinivas's
term[10]), or perhaps they simply wished to show respect for their
neighbors by not engaging in practices that the latter would find
offensive. The occupation of oil-presser and the concept of pollution that determined the relations between the Bene Israel and
Hindus made it difficult for the Bene Israel as a group, despite their
adoption of higher caste practices, to raise their status in the caste
hierarchy in the Konkan.

[10]According to Srinivas, Sanskritization is a process in which "a 'low' Hindu
caste or tribal or other group, changes its customs, ritual, ideology, and way of life
in the direction of a high, and frequently, 'twice-born' caste." Generally, such
changes are followed by a claim, made over a period of time, to a higher position
in the caste hierarchy. The upward movement of caste is marked by, among other
things, the banning of divorce and widow remarriage (Srinivas 1966:6, 7, 14, 148,
149).

Before the British came, the Konkan was dominated by Muslims much longer than by Hindus. During this period, the Bene Israel lived in very close harmony with the Muslims and shared their status. From the beginning of the twentieth century, however, "the Bene Israel derived their status not from their standing in Konkan society, but from their position in the cosmopolitan city of Bombay, [where] social status no longer derived from caste, but from class, which cut across caste or religious divisions" (Israel, personal communication, 6 Feb. 1979).

Even if one thinks of Indian Jews as a whole as a castelike group, one can also see the overtones of the caste system in the relationship within and between the Jewish communities themselves. The Cochin Jews had three endogamous castelike groups that did not interdine or intermarry. Bene Israel also distinguished between *kala* (black) and *gora* (white) Jews. In both cases, the question of ancestry, or descent, was important. The so-called white Jews considered the others "impure" because they were believed to descend from non-Jewish mothers or from those who had been converted. Although the concept of purity in this case is not the same as that in the true Indian caste sense, which refers to ritual purity and cleanliness, white Jews did not want black Jews near their cooking utensils. The Baghdadi Jews also adopted castelike attitudes toward the Bene Israel because of the latter's lack of ritual orthodoxy and supposed "ancestral impurity". In some, but not all, of these instances of "caste" distinctions among Jews, color played an important secondary role.[11]

Thus, in speaking of Jewish ethnic identity in India, one inevitably deals with caste. But superimposed on this traditional Indian structure was the British colonial presence, especially after 1857, when direct political rule over India was transferred from the British East India Company to the British crown (Cohn 1971:78).[12]

[11]Strizower (1971:30) talks of a "subcaste-like relationship" between *gora* and *kala*, pointing out that although they coexisted, they were not interdependent, and that *vis-a-vis* Indian society, they formed an undifferentiated group.

[12]Nathan Katz (personal communication, 30 Sept. 1987) has pointed out that British racism and Indian caste attitudes had an affinity that made British domination all the easier.

Jews in India now became British subjects.

The British presence affected the way in which the Jewish communities related to each other and to other Indian groups, the extent to which they identified with other Indians or with the colonial rulers, their attitudes toward Indian political aspirations, and their eventual relationship with Zionism. The position of the Jewish communities changed under the British so much that the eventual departure of the British greatly influenced the decision of Jews to remain in India or to leave.

When the Baghdadi or Iraqi Jews first arrived in Bombay, they were welcomed by the Bene Israel, who invited them to attend services in their synagogues and to bury their dead in the Bene Israel cemetery. The Baghdadis, in turn, tried to help the Bene Israel in their efforts to return to orthodoxy. Soon, however, a rift developed, the Baghdadis apparently deciding that the Bene Israel were very different from them after all (Fischel 1962:138-139). They were reluctant to intermarry with them and by the early twentieth century, began denying them certain rights in the synagogue. Bene Israel could not be counted to make up the *minyan* (quorum of ten males required for services to begin) in Baghdadi synagogues; nor were they called up to read certain prescribed portions of the Torah. They were excluded from Baghdadi charity trusts and burial grounds.[13] The Baghdadis apparently had some doubts as to the full "Jewishness" of the Bene Israel, partly because of their lack of observance of certain Jewish laws, particularly related to marriage, divorce and the ritual bath, partly because of their adoption of Hindu customs, and partly because the Baghdadis were not sure of the Bene Israel's Jewish ancestry. Some Baghdadis, however, used these doubts as a rationalization for their dissociation from the Bene Israel, a dissociation based more on racial, social and economic considerations

---

[13]Testimony of E.E. Moses, evidence, Rangoon Court Case (26 March 1935) 29-32; Office of the Sassoon Charity Trusts, Ballard Estate, Bombay, Trust deeds of the Jacob Sassoon Bombay Jewish Charity Fund (13 February 1899), of the Bombay Jewish Burial Ground (28 December 1908), of the Lady Rachel Sassoon Dispensary (12 December 1912), and of the Sir Jacob Sassoon Passover Food Trust Fund (18 December 1911).

than on religious concerns. The fair-complexioned Baghdadi Jews wished to assimilate to the ruling British and to be considered Europeans. In order to be fully accepted, they felt, they had to distance themselves from their darker, "native" brethren, the Bene Israel. The British denigration of Indians, superimposed on Indian conditions of caste and color, fostered the Baghdadis' inclination to distance themselves from the Bene Israel. The fact that in 1911, the Chief Rabbi Dr. Moses Gaster, head of the Sephardic Jews in England, wrote that he considered the Bene Israel to be very religious and good Jews and declared them to be "identical with the rest of the House of Israel," did not sway the Baghdadis.[14] In the 1930s, Baghdadi efforts to exclude Bene Israel from hospital beds reserved for Jews in Bombay and from participating in synagogue elections in Rangoon provoked the British Government's intervention in favour of the Bene Israel.[15]

The British analysis of Indian society was to have a profound impact not only on the Bene Israel but on the very nature of group identity in India. Louis Dumont, in discussing the caste system, talks about an ordered hierarchy in traditional India. He distinguishes between legitimacy derived from ritual status, which is hierarchical, and material success and power in the world, which is political. Ritual superiority does not mean secular or economic dominance. Castes were groups in society whose identity has been based on a fluid interaction with each other with "an overarching concept of hierarchy." The castes were ranked but not counted. In traditional society, they were fluid, not competing (Dumont 1980:xlviii, 4, 227-230, 258-260; see also Lelyveld 1986 and Srinivas 1966:30, 75). Bernard Cohn has discussed how the British, through a different analysis of Indian society, transformed these

---

[14]Gaster Papers, Moccatta Library, University College, London, letter from Gaster to I.E. Sargon (25 October 1911).

[15]Judgment in the High Court of Judicature at Rangoon, Original Civil Jurisdiction (9 April 1935). Civil Regular no. 85 of 1934. J.M. Ezekiel and one vs. C.S. Joseph and others. Published in *All India Law Reporter*, Rangoon Section (1935):6-8. Also, Government of Maharashtra, Archives, Elphinstone College, Bombay General Department, no. 1630/33 B.

hierarchically-ranked castes into competitive groups (Cohn 1963:13-15). The British saw caste as a concrete and measurable entity with "definable characteristics—endogamy, commensality rules, fixed occupation, common ritual practices." Castes could be counted, classified and ranked. Various ambitious castes now quickly perceived the chance of raising their status (Cohn 1963:15-18; see also Srinivas 1966:95-96).

The British not only created and enumerated categories of people, but used these categories for the allocation of patronage. Thus, the castes were no longer ranked and fluid, as in traditional India, but were now competing for educational resources and government employment. The castes also became the basis of political competition as representative institutions were introduced and as proportional representation developed in legislatures and offices.[16] This British analysis of society was relevant not only to Hindu castes, but to the non-Hindu minorities as well. Muslims, Christians, Anglo-Indians, Parsis, and Jews would eventually be classified and counted, and these numbers (as well as other factors) taken into consideration when it came to patronage.

In the first decades of the twentieth century, Hindu castes and ethnic groups throughout India began to form voluntary communal associations which promoted caste or group consciousness and tried to serve the general interest of the group. Among the Bene Israel, a number of organizations for communal improvement had already emerged by the end of the nineteenth century and their periodicals reflect their emerging consciousness as Jews with a civilization and culture different from that of other Indians (Lelyveld 1986:21; Srinivas 1966:92, 98; Cohn 1971:130; Israel 1963:12-13; and Strizower 1971:152). Writers questioned the Bene Israel assimilation of Hindu and Muslim customs and life-style and suggested that the Jews now begin to "separate out". In order to foster Jewish identity, the periodicals tried to present portraits of outstanding Jewish, particularly Anglo-Jewish personalities (*Israel Dharmadeep* 7, 15 March 1895:50).

---

[16]Castes claimed to be recorded in the census as a high caste and thus had a new, government-sponsored channel of caste mobility (Srinivas 1966:95-96).

The British not only named and classified castes and other groups, but treated them differently as regards employment. Distinctions were made between Indians and Europeans and among Indians themselves. In the lower ranks of certain public services, such as posts and telegraphs, police, customs, and railways, preferences were given to Anglo-Indians, Christians, Parsis and Jews, who were thought to be more reliable than Hindus and Muslims. Many Bene Israel thus gravitated to these jobs and found economic security within the British civil services (*Israel Dharmadeep* 4, 1 May 1885:143-144; Israel, interview, 28 December 1977; and Schermerhorn 1978:218-219).

Therefore as Indian nationalism developed in the first half of the twentieth century, the Bene Israel were ambivalent. They constantly expressed their gratitude and loyalty to Great Britain. Many Bene Israel, dependent on the British for employment, were reluctant to support Indian nationalism too strongly. Yet they remained aware that, throughout their history, India was the one country that had not persecuted Jews. Most saw themselves as Indian and identified with other Indians. Some of the leading members of the community, highly placed professionals, were proud to be Indian and sympathized with the aspirations of Indian nationalists. They felt it would be unwise to tie themselves too closely to England, as the split would eventually come. But most Bene Israel were political fence-sitters; pro-British in their heart of hearts, they only turned to nationalism gradually. By 1947, most of the Bene Israel in India had become staunchly pro-Gandhi, but the development had been a slow and natural process.[17]

During the period that Baghdadis and Bene Israel struggled to work out their relationship to each other and to Indian nationalism, the growth of Zionism opened up yet another channel of identity.

---

[17]*The Bene Israel Conference Imbroglio*, a letter to the Bene Israel community by Jacob B. Israel, Abraham S.Erulkar, D.G. Samson, and Aaron Benjamin (Bombay, 1 December 1917); *Friend of Israel* 2 (November 1917): 131-133; 2 (December 1917): 142-144; 4(March-April 1919):24; J.B. Israel, *Letter to the Bene Israel Community of British India* (Bombay, 1917-18); B.J. Israel, interviews (30 November 1977 and 21 December 1977).

Far removed from the centers of Jewish life, the Jews of India were nevertheless aware of events affecting their co-religionists elsewhere, such as the persecution of Jews of eastern Europe after World War I, and the British occupation of Palestine and its implication for the future of world Jewry. The Central Zionist offices, eager to reach out to Jewish communities all over the world, initiated contact with India. Now the Jews of India were faced with the same dilemmas as Jews everywhere: Would they see themselves as simply a religious minority in the country they had inhabited for so long, or would they shift gears and define themselves as part of an ethnic "nation" that needed a home of its own? Many Bene Israel showed some interest in Zionism, although they were uncertain how it would directly affect them. Others, however, disturbed by the way in which the Bene Israel had been viewed by other Jews in the past, had reservations. Would they be considered full Jews in a Jewish state? Behind this question was the implication that Indian Jews would do better to see themselves first as Indians, rather than as Jews.[18]

Events in Europe in the 1930s confirmed the reality of the Indian Jews' links with the wider Jewish community. The rise of Hitler and Nazi anti-Semitism forged a heightened sense of solidarity with their suffering brethren, a number of whom were now arriving on Indian shores. Hindu and Muslim nationalists, now in a position to make the fulfilment of their demands the condition for full cooperation with the British during the war, had reservations about the war effort. In contrast, minority groups such as the Anglo-Indians and the Jews were more supportive. The Jews of India displayed the same loyalty to the Allies as Jews elsewhere. There was simply no choice. For most Bene Israel, their identification with their persecuted coreligionists and their overriding loyalty to the British outweighed any identification with Indian nationalism they might have had. Their sense of an ethnic identity within India

[18]*Israelite* 3 (1919):74, 101-102, 115, 123; 4 (1920):59; Central Zionist Archives (Jerusalem) Z 4/2472; *Third and Fourth Bene Israel Conference Reports*, 1919-1920 (Bombay, 1922):8-12, 75-76.

had now developed into an ethnic consciousness that encompassed Jews around the world.

Thus, the challenges confronting the Jews of India in the nineteenth and twentieth centuries—British rule and the opportunities it made available, the nationalist movement, and the resurgence of their Judaism, and Zionism—were closely interrelated. These challenges seemed to point to three options for the Jews as an ethnic group in the postwar period: a communal cultural autonomy within a pluralistic, egalitarian, independent India; a greater affirmation of their ethnicity through the espousal of Zionism and emigration to Israel; and emigration to other countries.

The emergence of an independent Israel was an enormous lure. The economic uncertainties expected for all Indians after independence, coupled with the special opportunity for emigration provided by the birth of the State of Israel, enticed many Jews to leave. But it was the strong sense of an ethnic Jewish consciousness that had developed during the British Raj that enabled them to embrace this option.

One cannot help speculating whether the partition of the subcontinent into two religiously determined states did not in some way affect the thinking of Indian Jews about the relationship between religion and territory as an element of communal identity.[19] It is certainly possible that had Zionism and the State of Israel not afforded an alternative, the Bene Israel would have remained as an ethnic group in a pluralistic, independent India.

Looking from the perspective of comparative Jewish history, one is struck by the uniqueness of the Bene Israel story. Starting as a castelike group in villages within a hierarchically organized society, having little contact with the Jewish world beyond India, they had become increasingly religiously observant and had iden-

[19]Dumont (1980:331) has pointed out: "The notion of a common territory appears so necessary in the modern consciousness of political identity that it is most unlikely that things might have taken another turn...[Territory] is generally considered a *sine qua non* of the realization of a nation, while other elements, a common history..., a common culture, a common language, are more or less frequently found, but are not indispensable."

tified themselves with Jewish ethnicity and world Jewry, without experiencing the anti-Semitism felt elsewhere in the world. Even the emergence of Israel and independent India's pro-Arab tilt had hardly affected their position. Their emigration to Israel was conditioned not, as in many Muslim countries, by a persecution resulting from the creation of the State of Israel, but by an attraction to the Holy Land and an uncertainty about postcolonial India.

The central issue for the Bene Israel, and indeed for all Jews of India today, is the very survival of their community. With perhaps only five thousand Jews remaining in India and forty to fifty thousand Jews of Indian descent now living in Israel, their institutions in India are struggling to remain alive. Synagogues and prayer halls are gradually closing or finding their membership shrinking. One cannot be certain whether the tiny remnants of Jews in India will be able to preserve the special character and heritage of their communities, nor whether a distinctive identity can be maintained by the Indian Jews already in Israel.

Sources cited

Cohn, Bernard S. 1963. "Notes on the History of the Study of Indian Society and Culture", pp. 13-15 in Milton Singer and Bernard S. Cohn, eds., *Structure and Change in Indian Society.* Chicago: University of Chicago Press.

——————. 1971. *India: The Social Anthropology of a Civilization.* Englewood Cliffs, NJ: Prentice-Hall.

Dumont, Louis. 1980. *Homo Hierarchicus: The Caste System and Its Implications.* Chicago and London: University of Chicago Press.

Fischel, Walter J. 1972. "Bombay in Jewish History in the Light of New Documents from the Indian Archives", *Proceedings of the American Academy of Jewish Research* 38-39:119-44.

Godbey, Allen H. 1930. *The Lost Tribes: A Myth.* Durham, NC: Duke University Press.

Isenberg, Shirley B. 1988, *India's Bene Israel: A Comprehensive Inquiry and Sourcebook.* Bombay: Popular Prakashan and

Berkeley: Judah L. Magnes Museum.

Israel, Benjamin J. 1963. *Religious Evolution among the Bene Israel of India since 1750.* Bombay: The author.

——————. 1982. *The Jews of India.* New Delhi: Centre for Jewish and Interfaith Studies, Jewish Welfare Association.

——————. 1984. *The Bene Israel of India: Some Studies.* New York: Apt Books.

Joseph, Brenda. 1986. "Samaji's Synagogue: Tales and Traditions", pp. 361-366 in Thomas A. Timberg ed., *Jews in India.* New York: Apt Books.

Kehimkar, Hayeem S. 1937. *The History of the Bene Israel in India.* Tel Aviv: Dayag.

Lelyveld, David. 1986. "Fissiparous Tendencies and All that: Parts and Wholes in Modern India." Draft paper presented at China-Harvard Seminar, J.K. Fairbanks East Asian Research Center, Harvard University, 11 April.

Roth, Cecil. 1941. *The Sassoon Dynasty.* London: Robert Hale Ltd.

Samuel, Shellim. 1963. *Treatise on the Origin and Early History of the Beni-Israel of Maharashtra State.* Bombay: Iyer & Iyer.

Schermerhorn, R.A. 1978. *Ethnic Plurality in India.* Tucson: University of Arizona Press.

Srinivas, M.N. 1966. *Social Change in Modern India.* Berkeley: University of California Press.

Strizower, Schifra. 1971. *The Bene Israel of Bombay: A Study of a Jewish Community.* New York: Schocken.

Timberg, Thomas A., ed. 1986. *Jews in India.* New York: Apt Books.

Weil, Shalva. 1977. "Names and Identity among the Bene Israel," *Ethnic Groups* 1:201-219.

Wilson, John. 1847. *Lands of the Bible.* Edinburgh: William Whyte and Co.

——————. 1854. *Appeal for the Christian Education of the Bene Israel.* Bombay: No publisher listed. Also Edinburgh, 1852 and 1865.

Part III

The Baghdadi Jews

5

Indigenous and Non-Indigenous Jews

Thomas A. Timberg

The outlook of most religious groups contains both social and intellectual elements. Most adherents probably value the latter more than the former. But in certain religions, such as Judaism, these elements are explicitly fused. Traditional rabbinic Judaism is based on a covenant between a particular social group and the deity, what Adin Steinsaltz has recently called "a contract without an escape clause." (Steinsaltz 1990).

Religious and cultural identity are thus fused for religious Jews, though not for secular ones. In fact, this fusion accounts for some of the otherwise difficult-to-understand positions of those Jews who are influenced by mysticism. This applies both to those who are thought of as of the right, such as the Lubavitcher Rebbe or Rav Kook, and those on the left like Solomon Shechter. These positions are based on a sanctity accorded to the Jewish people as such by this contract "without an escape clause."

At one extreme the Jews are quintessentially "the people who stand alone" and the people who "avoid the customs of the non-Jew". As Haman phrases it in the *Book of Esther* (4:8), "There is a certain people scattered abroad and dispersed among the people in all the provinces of thy kingdom, and their laws are diverse from those of every people."

This does not mean that a Jew cannot be a good citizen of the state, giving to it because it gives to him or her. The rabbis of the Talmud developed a social contract concept which legitimated the primarily non-Jewish state. As is recorded in the *Ethics of the Fathers*, "Rabbi Hanina, the deputy of the priests said: 'Pray for the peace of the government, for except for the fear of that we should have swallowed each other alive" (*Pirke Avoth* 1971).[1] However, for two thousand years Jews have done more. They have taken on partially or fully the cultural identity of the larger non-Jewish communities among whom they lived. They became German, French, or American Jews. Sometimes the identity was not the majority one. The Jews of Eastern Europe, like much of its elite, spoke a Germanic language among a Slavic majority; the bulk of those in Greece and Turkey, a Hispanic one. In general, until the modern period Jews remained remarkably impervious to the intellectual trends in the cultures in which they lived. Though Greek philosophy was assimilated, they were remarkably uniterested in the religious developments that surrounded them. This is certainly the case for the Jews of Indian in general, as I have shown elsewhere (Timberg 1985:6).

This cultural isolation was not inconsistent with a high degree of civic loyalty and even virtue. But this sort of "social contract" loyalty was not sufficient after the rise of modern nationalism. All of the world's main religions have sat uncomfortably with the demands of this nationalism. It was harder to give to "Caesar" what was his due, when that was defined in unlimited terms.

A. The Baghdadi Jews of India

In what follows I describe how a Jewish group, the Baghdadi Jews of India, dealt with the rise of modern nationalism. They were one among the units of a Baghdadi or Iraqi Diaspora extending from London to Shanghai, which operated to a considerable extent as ancillary to the British trading networks at least from the mid-nineteenth century onward, as well as playing an important part in India's economy. Baghdadi should be taken in its broadest sense. Actually Basra, Baghdad's port, was a more important source than Baghdad itself for the Indian migration. Shalom Ovadya HaCohen,

---

[1]The perception is analogous to the New Testament injunction in *Romans* 13:1-7.

the founder of the Calcutta community, in fact came from Aleppo and because he was the founder of the Calcutta community, it continued to follow various Aleppo—i.e. North Syrian—rituals, even though most of its members came from Iraq. The Baghdadi Jews' economic and social role changed as did their own status from alien pioneers, to key commercial interlocutors for the British, to a final role as a prosperous but peripheral part of the Indian economy.

The population figures we have are a little shaky. The Calcutta figures are as follows:

Census	Jews	Armenians
		(for comparison)
1816	50	
1822-23	100	
1837	300	
1841	636	
1866	681	703
1876	952	576
1881	982	892
1891	1387	557
1901	1919	792
1911	1920	832
1921	1820	987
1931	1830	738
1951	1945	
1961	1191	

There was a steady increase until 1901, stability until Indian independence, and rapid decline thereafter. The Armenian pattern is roughly comparable. The Census recorded forty-eight Jews in 1971 and none in 1981, but these figures are clearly inaccurate. A recent court case determined that there were over 100 Jews in Calcutta in the mid-1980s (Timberg 1985).

Baghdadi Jews were not separately enumerated in Bombay, but were enumerated along with another group, the Bene Israel Jews. Baghdadis were estimated to have numbered 350 in 1837 and to have reached 2910 by 1941—by so classifying all the Jewish residents of Baghdadi Jewish neighborhoods, a presumption which is not accurate (Isenberg: 279-306).

They had originally traded on their own account with the ports of the Persian Gulf and their names appear in connection with this trade in 1840s. The earliest traders in Surat (the West Indian entrepot before Bombay), Bombay, and Calcutta were prominent as traders in gems, Arabian horses, and rose water. Shalom Ovadya Hacohen (1762-1836, first of Surat then of Calcutta) was court jeweller to the Nawab of Oudh in the early nineteenth century, as well as the head of the Jewish community in Calcutta (Timberg 1985). Shalom Ovadya and one of his sons-in-law served as spiritual leaders and left us, in both cases, extensive diaries.

Soon opium became the staple items of trade for Jews—as it did for many other Indians—after the British victory in the Opium War with China in 1842, and a second victory in 1860 which forced the opening of the Chinese market. The opium produced in India was exchanged for tea in China which, in turn was shipped to England to permit India to pay for its imports from England and for the services of the Englishmen who ruled it (Timberg 1985:277-278, 28ff; Musleah 1975:17-38; Ezra 1986). Many of the leading fortunes of all communities in nineteenth-century India were made in this opium trade.

As the opium trade declined—partly because of government policy—the traders moved to cotton and jute, which followed it as export staples. The two branches of the house of David Sassoon in Bombay extended their activities backward from the cotton trade, building docks and handling facilities for cotton exports and cotton mills to manufacture yarn and cloth. By the end of the nineteenth century the two firms between them owned the largest number of cotton textile mills in India of any industrial group.

Other Jewish firms continued trading in various other commodities more so from Calcutta than Bombay. Sassoon J. David was among the leading founders of the Central Bank of India in Bombay; B.N. Elias made his fortune in commodity markets before and during the First World War, and went on to found a business group which owned a jute mill, a major cigarette company, a large hotel and real estate interests, as well as continuing trading interests. Yet other Jewish firms, with or without non-Jewish partners, were involved in the stock exchange, bone mills, etc.

Corresponding to these large, often intermarried families of successful businessmen there emerged a middle and a lower class, who worked for the former and ran their own smaller businesses, sometimes living on the charity of the successful business class. The community was better organized in Bombay than in Calcutta, so a better charity net was available. In both cities, but more so in Calcutta, there were Jews at all levels of the economic and social structure.

Ezra gives the census report of Jewish professions in Calcutta from the 1901 *Census*.[2] There were 511 employed males and sixty-nine females employed in ninety-eight different professions: Thirty-one men and women were piece goods dealers, eleven men and five women were tailors, twenty-five men were carpenters, nineteen stationers, twenty-three men and three women were general merchants and seventy-one men worked in other mercantile establishments; twenty-four men and two women were shopkeepers, seventeen men were peddlers, forty-two men were brokers and agents, and nineteen men and thirty women lived on rents and investments. On the other hand, twenty men and six women were domestic servants, ten men "ministers of religion", and sixteen men and four women were teachers. Seven women were prostitutes, seven men and five women singers and actors, three were piano tuners, and one a bandmaster. Six men were diplomaed doctors, six lawyers, and one a civil engineer. It is likely from what one knows of the period that most of the categories, from the prostitutes onward, were European Jews (Ezra 1986:452-453). Precise details of this sort for Bombay are harder to come by because the Baghdadi figures there are mixed with those of the Bene Israel to a considerable extent.

Fleeing originally from persecutions such as those of Daud Pasha in Baghdad in 1817-31 and the forcible conversion of the

---

[2]These figures include a few non-Baghdadi Jews, especially Europeans.

Meshed Jews in Persia in 1839, these Jews found refuge in India. David Sassoon (1792-1864), who had been leader of the community in Baghdad, arrived in Bombay in 1833, Joseph ben Ezra ben Joseph (Khleif) in Calcutta in 1820 and Mulla Ibrahim Nathan (d. 1868) in Bombay in 1844 (Timberg 1985:275; Musleah 1975:48, 168-179, 300, 310).

They arrived with strong ties not only to their own Baghdadi Diaspora but to the British as well. Mulla Ibrahim had served the British as an agent in Central Asia (Fischel 1970: 178-198). Their attitude is best indicated by a note on a leaf in a prayerbook from Meshed written immediately after the forcible conversion in 1839 and quoted by Fischel:

> Now there is no hope for us except first, all the mercies of the Holy One Blessed be He, second, the King Messiah, and third, that the English come.... The Holy one, Blessed be He, in his gracious glory which over us in mercy and save us from this exile of Ishmael (1970:179).

Socially, the better off Jews who led the community were rapidly integrated with British society. Of David Sassoon's eight sons, all but one moved to England (Timberg 1985). David Sassoon's eldest son, Sir Albert Abdallah Bt. (1818-1896), transferred his business headquarters there in the 1880s. Of his other sons, Sassoon David had left for England before 1867, and Reuben and Arthur, who also moved to England early in life became associated with the Prince of Wales, the future Edward VII. Only Solomon David remained in Bombay, where he managed the main family firm from 1877 until his death in 1894. After his death, his widow, Flora, managed the firm until 1901 when she moved to England and became a major figure in Jewish community affairs there until her death in 1936. All of the eight brothers of Sir David Ezra (1871-1947), the leading figure in the Calcutta Jewish community of his generation, moved to England. E. Meyer, another magnate from Calcutta settled in England sometimes in the first decade of the twentieth century (Timberg 1985). Even those who stayed in India

often saw their children and grandsons leave. Sir Sassoon J. David
Bt. (1849-1926, no immediate relation of the Sassoons, but married
to a grand-daughter of David Sassoon), saw his son Sir Perceval
David, most prominent as a Chinese art collector, settled in London
(Timberg 1985). Those members of the elite who remained in India
took long vacations in England, adopted the English dress, language, and manners and were progressively accepted as marginal
members of the European community for many purposes—though
in the caste-ridden society of Anglo-India it was always clear that
they did not quite belong (Godden 1982). Ruth Fredman Cornea in
a companion piece in this volume makes the point very succinctly.
The social shift was marked by a change of residence from the old
Jewish quarter to the European area (Timberg 1985:28-45; Ezra
1986:441-448).

We have some excellent nostalgic accounts of the kind of life
the middle and upper classes lived in Calcutta in two fond memoirs
by those who were part of it, as well as now in a best-selling novel,
(Elias 1974, Ezra 1986, Courter 1990). As usual, there is less
documentation from Bombay; the two pieces I am familiar with are
fleeting glimpses of school life and a couple of memoirs by David
Sassoon the Second (Judah 1967). Anglicization was less complete
farther down the social structure, but the community was led and
dominated by its elite, mercantile elements.

Several travellers emphasized in thier memoirs the social gaps
between the elite and masses. My own impressions of the community in its last days would certainly confirm this. But as a counter it
is useful to look at the family trees reproduced in volume two of
Esmond Ezra's memoirs. He is descended from Shalom Ovadya
HaCohen and is related to many prominent as well as humble
families in the community. The family trees cover 2,500 people,
admittedly not all of them Calcuttan or even Jewish, but they also
omit a large number of prominent people, many of whom are
referred to in the text. I think what is reflected is a largely middle
class community tending toward the prosperous, with a considerable number of very wealthy and a few poor members. The Bombay
community may have had a slightly different composition because

of the dominating role of the Sassoons but this is hard to verify, as I noted above.

In Calcutta, there was a movement of protest against this dominance of a few wealthy families led by Ezra Arakie (1875-1942), a barrister and Cambridge graduate (Timberg 1985, and Ezra 1986:393-430). He took over the leadership of Naveh Shalom Synagogue, a membership organization unlike the other synagogues which were controlled by trustees. The record indicates that the wealthier congregations in the other synagogues set expenditure standards that the poorer members who formed Naveh Shalom could not meet in matters like charitable donations. The division extended to the matter of schools. Ezra Arakie's free Talmud Torah coexisted uncomfortably with the Jewish Girls School run by Rev E.M.D. Cohen, the Rabbi of David Ezra's Maghen David. The struggles between this synagogue and Naveh Shalom located in the older Maghen David Synagogue which it abutted eventually led to a series of cases which were carried up to the Privy Council in London, the highest court of appeal for Indian cases. The division was complex since we note that many of the wealthy in the community figured among the supporters of Arakie's school and the Naveh Shalom party and Arakie himself clearly belonged to the community elite. There seems to have been less of protest in Bombay. The dominating role of the Sassoon Trusts and firms meant that there was little organized dissension in the Baghdadi community. In Calcutta, where no one family dominated, and where there were a number of people not under the cover of the community welfare network, dissension seems to have been endemic.

The cultural Anglicization naturally led to an attenuation of the connection of the elite, and thus of the community with their "home" Arabic-speaking communities. The brief efflorescence of Hebraeo-Arabic newspapers in the late nineteenth century in Calcutta and Bombay was soon over (Timberg 1985). Figures such as the first David Sassoon and Haham Shlomo Tweyna in Calcutta, who exerted cultural as well as economic influence throughout the Arabic-speaking Jewish world and beyond, soon passed from the scene (Timberg 1985). India continued to be an important source of funding for Baghdadi charities and a refuge for Baghdadis even in the early 1940s. The period when the Judahs in Calcutta were the major financiers of Porat Yosef, the leading Sephardic academic institution in Jerusalem, was soon over. The Jewish educational standards of the Jewish elite fell dramatically. A solid institutional network was eventually set up in both Bombay and Calcutta for the poor and the education of poorer Jewish children, but (with the partial exception of the Jewish Girls' School in Calcutta) not for the children of the wealthy who were sent to the best English schools in India (Timberg 1985).

The Baghdadis were largely unaffected by the creeds of their Indian neighbors. It was rather the Christian missionaries with their European aura who presented a challenge, especially in Calcutta where the welfare network was weak. Of course, there were scattered intermarriages and conversions to Judaism; the two most prominent I know of were from Hindu families.

The most interesting story concerns Abhijit Guha, a leading nineteenth century Calcutta lawyer, who converted to Judaism and raised his two daughters as Jews. He also paid for the education of the two young Baghdadis who were intended as marriage partners for his daughters. The young men eventually refused, but the daughters went on to lead influential lives. One, Hannah Guha Sen, married Dr. Arun Sen, a leading physician in Delhi, and went on to become Principal of Lady Irwin College. She was active in the Indian women's movement and in Jewish affairs until her death. Her grandson is today a prominent professor in Delhi. A branch of the Paikpara Raj, leading Bengali landowners, converted and continue as active Jews in London.

Some of the Baghdadi Jewish institutional network was created to counter missionary efforts (Timberg 1985). The Jewish school in Calcutta was reorganized on a sound footing in 1907, but it was only in 1918 that its enrolment exceeded that of the Christian Hebrew Mission School which was closed only in 1922. I cannot imagine that anti-missionary impulses did not also spur the creation of the Bombay Jewish school, but cannot find explicit documentation.

Before the Zionist movement made its presence felt in India in the 1920s, there was little intellectual contact with other non-

Baghdadi Indian Jews. Cochini and Malabari Jews (so-called white and black Jews) were welcome in Baghdadi communities, and the Bene Israel, as well apparently, in Calcutta. One of the early histories of the Calcutta community is written by a Bene Israel who worked there as a journalist (Isaac 1917). The Rangoon situation with its rejection of other groups of Jews, is described at some length by Cernea in this volume. The Cochinis, with a particularly high level of Jewish education but less in the way of large scale business interests, played an important role as printers and teachers for Baghdadis and other Jews. In Bombay, after an initial period when the Baghdadis apparently shared synagogues and certainly cemeteries, the Maratha-speaking Bene Israel were explicitly excluded by the Baghdadi community. This exclusion clearly began in the 1860s and reached its height around the First World War. There continued to be some moving back and forth, and several leaders of the community, including the Sassoons gave funds to Bene Israel institutions. Two Bene Israel became headmasters of the Baghdadi English medium shcool and many Bene Israel found work in the Sassoon mills (Strizower 1971:42-48, 67-71; Israel 1984:53-87; Roland 1989:128-146).

The Baghdadi elite were not only assimilated to English norms, they had a tendency to move to England. They were replaced by a newly monied elite. The emigration of the elite meant that there was some role for the middle class, and their activity expanded. At the same time, several Baghdadi Jews played important roles in the general Indian scene—the aforementioned Hannah Sen, founder of Lady Irwin College in Delhi, Gen. J.F.K. Jacobs in the Army, Ezra Mir in documentary films, and several film actresses, particularly Sulochana (Ruby Meyers) and Nadeera.

A certain amount of Zionist activity also took place. Baghdadis were quite active in the Zionist movement in India (Musleah 1975:414-420; and Roland 1990:128-146). Of some interest is the role of Albert Menasseh and his associates in spearheading the revival of orthodoxy among some Baghdadis and of the Ezras, Percy Gourgey, and the Sargons in Bombay Zionism (Timberg 1985; Roland 1989).

B. Baghdadis and Indianness

Whether the Baghdadis are indigenous or not is essentially a matter of interpretation. Indigeneity in the South Asian subcontinent is a complex phenomenon. The traditional social system in which a number of largely endogamous castes and communities relate to each other lends a certain "foreignness" to all such communities. To quote something I wrote two decades ago:

> "The description by Weber of a pariah people as a 'distinctive hereditary social group' and as having 'distinctiveness' in economic function; was generally characteristic of all Indian castes and communities. It thus hardly differentiates entrepreneurial groups from the others. *In this sense, India may be considered a continent of pariah peoples.*" (Timberg 1978).

The major Indian Jewish communities are endogamous units. Among the Bene Israel there were traditionally endogamous, *gora* and *kala* groups, though the latter was very small and have disappeared. Among the Cochin Jews both the Paradesi ("white" Cochini) and Malabari ("black") Jews were endogamous and neither intermarried with the two separate hereditary groups of *meshuchrarim* (freedmen) who generally worshipped with them, although they were discriminated against. The main groups of Bene Israel and Cochin, as well as the Baghdadis—all emphasized their foreign origin.

They did not differ so much in this respect from the major Hindu groups as a whole. All of upper caste Hindudom claims descent from the Aryan invaders who came pouring over the passes from Afghanistan and displaced whatever indigenous peoples they found. More particularly, various Hindu castes and tribes have more specific origin stories. The Namboodiri Brahmins of Kerala and the Chitpavans of the Konkan littoral claim, just like the Bene Israel, that their ancestors had been shipwrecked and washed ashore, and were revived by their partron deity.

But the question of indigeneity is particularly relevant to

Baghdadi Jews because of the impression that their "foreignness" is particularly pronounced. In contrast with the Bene Israel and Cochinis, neither traditional language, dress, or cuisine had anything in common with the majority of those among whom they lived. As time progressed they abandoned the Arabic language and customs which they shared with other small groups of port city "foreigners" for the English and Hindustani which were the *lingua franca* of those cities.

In the beginning, the "mother" cultural group for the Baghdadis was the Baghdadi Jewish trading Diaspora, which stretched east from Baghdad to China and Japan, and west to London. Later, the "mother" culture was the English-speaking community centered on London and in particular its Jewish subset; and finally, a part of the Jewish community centered on Israel. There were always strong elements of identification with India and Indian culture, certainly an active civic participation in the life of the port metropolis as there were individuals with a strong sense of Indian identity.

C. Transition

There has been a natural transition in the Baghdadi community's history from a Judaeo-Arabic cultural identity to an Indo-Anglian one. There are parallels of such transition among a number of the so-called "gray town" communities—Armenians, Greeks, Iranians, etc. These communities are so named because in the eighteenth and early nineteenth century they lived in the middle, between the "blacktown" of the "native" Indians and the "white town" of the British. Economically they fitted into various niches—especially as urban landlords—and socially they were assimilated into the British community. By the twentieth century, their legal and to a considerable extent their social status had merged with that of people of Britain, which became their cultural center.

I documented this process in Calcutta, where it was particularly pronounced, in an article reprinted in a recent book on Jews in India. The process differed in detail in Bombay but the process in the two cities had much in common. The relative importance of Armenians and Greeks in Bombay was much less, particularly by the nine-teenth century. The Baghdadi Jewish presence in Bombay was large but dominated—socially and financially—by the two branches of the House of Sassoon, which meant there were fewer political and factional conflicts than in Calcutta, and thus much less in the way of historic "events" and public records.

As far as Baghdadi Jews in Bombay were concerned, the pressure of British culture was somewhat less intense, not the least because of the presence of a somewhat larger, neutral, cultural realm populated by the westernized Parsees, and several of the Portuguese-named Christian communities, Goans, Mangaloreans, and East Indians (who came from the area around Bombay). Further, the commercial dominance of the British was much less, and a large amount of business was dependent on Indian firms.

However, a detailed study of the differences in acculturation is difficult. As noted already, the absence of conflict in Bombay has meant a lack of historical record. Whereas the Calcutta Jewish community has produced at least five full-length histories, there are none of the Bombay Baghdadi Jews. There is some documentation of the Bombay community (Sassoon 1949, Yaakov 1965, Fischel 1970, Roth 1941, Jackson 1968). There is little in the way of census data—because the data is not given separately for Bene Israel and Baghdadis for the later censuses, and the records of the Baghdadi community itself are unavailable for the period before 1914—all this in marked contrast to Calcutta.

D. Some Parallels

Two other parallels are worth examining: (1) the Baghdadi communities in non-Indian settings namely in Singapore, Penang, Shanghai, Hong Kong and Rangoon; and (2) the Jewish communi-ties in the major centers of the Middle East (Kranzler 1989, Leventhal 1985). Jewish settlements in Baghdad and Damascus have dated from time immemorial but the Jewish settlements in Cairo and Beirut are far more recent. Despite the existence of an ancient and medieval Jewish settlement in Cairo, the modern community there largely consisted of recent immigrants.

All the British colonial entrepot Jewish communities had roughly parallel experiences. The pole of European colonial culture was a hard one to avoid. A 1989 work by Gudrun Kramer deals with the issue at some length:

> By adopting, even if superficially, European culture and education, the Jewish upper and middle classes moved away and became alienated both from their Jewish background and Egyptian environment. The adoption of European languages and first names was only the most visible sign of this new orientation and gradual integration into the cosmopolitan subculture which was particularly strong in Alexandria. On the economic level, the Jewish middle and upper classes were closely linked to and indeed identified with, the economic system established and upheld by the colonial power. On the political level, the Jewish elite stressed its loyalty to the Egyptian nation and the king, but barely participated in the national struggle.[3]
> The dynamics and Westernization of the Jewish middle and upper classes, which proved so useful in the economic sphere, manoeuvred them into a marginal, and ultimately precarious position within Egyptian society at large. If this offered them a chance to serve as intermediaries between Egypt and Europe, especially in the economic sphere, it also exposed them as dependents of Britain and the colonial system in general. These ties made them part of European and Levantine local foreign colonies, regardless of their origin and nationality (Kramer 1989:230-231).

This kind of cultural assimilation, of necessity, had to have an impact on the religious identity of the Baghdadi Jews, for whom religion, nationality and culture are inextricably linked, as for Jews

---

[3]The last is a mis-statement as demonstrated elsewhere in the book. Considering their small size and relatively limited influence, one might say the Jewish were disproportionately active, particularly in parties of the Left.

everywhere. In India, in contrast to the United States and the United Kingdom, or even among the Bene Israel (another Jewish group in India), this did not result in a movement for religious reform but the pressure of cultural assimilation was very powerful.

Of course, there was a tendency to have religious forms Anglicized. Those attending synagogues were to wear ties, suits, and buttoned up shoes rather than the flowing robes and slippers of their ancestors. Though older cuisine was conserved, there was a greater use of English dishes, and adoption of English eating times. Some of this was enforced by the government. There was pressure to use coffins, as in Europe; slavery and polygamy became illegal. Jews were subject to the Indian Marriages Act as affirmed in the landmark Abraham v. Abraham case in 1856, with its painfully difficult procedures for divorce, rather than the more liberal traditional Jewish legislation.

But the leadership of the community continued to be strictly orthodox, and guaranteed that community organizations were orthodox as well. Some of this might be attributed to the personal predilections of members of the older generation. In fact, it was the more observant members of the wealthy families who stayed in India, whereas the less observant tended to emigrate to England. Solomon David Sassoon and his sons became the one really orthodox branch of the house of Sassoon, and the ones who retained their Indian connections the longest. Sir Sassoon J. David remained rigorously pious; his son Sir Perceval moved to England and took less interest in either India or Judaism. Sir David Ezra, the leader of the Calcutta community, was rigidly pious, and the only one of the several brothers who remained in India.

Of course, we are dealing with a self-reinforcing phenomenon. The more observant control the community and thus are happier staying on in the country. The challenges to the community leadership were not as much for religious reform as they were for greater observance.

The rank and file of the community did become less observant. Although this undoubtedly had a marginal effect, it had remarkably little impact on community institutions. I would suggest that the general Indian environment, in which other communities also adhered to orthodox creeds—while sufficient tolerance permitted the non-observant to remain affiliated—may have facilitated this general orthodoxy. Joan Roland suggests that in Bombay the orthodoxy may possibly have been a "marker" as well, to defferentiate Baghdadis from Europeans and Bene Israel, but it could have been, and to some extent was, a basis for affiliation between individual Baghdadis and the Bene Israel. The yeshiva in Bombay and several business partnerships in Calcutta were based on just such affiliations.

E. Today

Whatever the case, the Baghdadi community has almost ceased to exist in India; probably less than 250 individuals each are living in Calcutta and Bombay today, most of them either quite elderly or estranged from the community or at least its religious institutions. Synagogues continue to function, though none maintains the daily prayer quorum they had until the mid-1980s. This is, however, not a direct result of the cultural orientation of Indian Baghdadi Jews but more of the loss of some of the economic functions which they had traditionally performed, together with the attractions of emigration.

There are, of course, reconstituted Baghdadi communities in places like London and Australia, with strong Indian constituents. But as the generations pass these are declining as well, and the children tend to join the broader mainstream, Jewish and otherwise. Some of this is illustrated by the numerous family trees which form part of Esmond Ezra's memoir (Ezra 1986). However, the point to be made in the end is that the "foreignness" of the Baghdadi's was not a disturbing element in traditional Indian society, with its easy tolerance of, but compartmentalization of differences, just as it was not a disturbing element in the millet society of the pre-modern Middle East. But the new secular nationalism which characterizes the modern sector of Indian society delegitimizes the particularism a separate Jewish cultural identity implies—as it does all communal identities.

Thus it is as difficult in the contemporary period in Westernized Bombay or Calcutta to maintain a separate culture as it is in most of the Western societies themselves—and the cultural challenges and issues are roughly the same. There are pressures on the remaining younger Jews to fit in, and to maintain their cultural peculiarity is, in some sense, a burden.

Sources cited

Blanc, Haim. 1964. *Communal Dialects in Baghdad.* Cambridge, MA: Harvard University Press.

Courter, Virginia. 1990. *Flowers in the Blood.* New York: Dutton.

Elias, Flower. 1974. *The Jews of Calcutta: The Autobiography of a Community: 1798-1972.* Calcutta: The Jewish Association of Calcutta.

Ezra, Esmond. 1986. *Turning Back the Pages: A Chronicle of Calcutta Jewry.* 3 vols. London: Brookside Press.

Fischel, Walter J. 1970. *Hayehudium b'Hodu.* Jerusalem: Ben Zvi Institute. [in Hebrew]

Godden, Rumer. 1982. *The Dark Horse.* New York: Viking Press.

Isaac, I.A. 1917. *A Short Account of the Calcutta Jews, with a Sketch of the Bene-Israels, the Cochin Jews, the Chinese Jews and the Black Jews of Abyssinia.* Calcutta: The author.

Isenberg, Shirley B. 1988. *India's Bene Israel: A Comprehensive Inquiry and Sourcebook.* Bombay: Popular Prakashan.

Israel, Benjamin J. 1984. *The Bene Israel of India: Some Studies.* Bombay: Orient Longmans. [original publication:1963. *Religious Evolution among the Bene Israel of Bombay since 1750.* Bombay: I.S. Shapurkar.]

Jackson, Stanley. 1968. *The Sassoons,* New York: Dutton.

Judah, Aaron. 1967. *Clown on Fire.* New York: Dial Press.

Kramer, Gudrun. 1989. *The Jews in Modern Egypt: 1914-1952.* Seattle: University of Washington Press.

Kranzler, David. 1979. *Japanese, Nazis, and Jews.* New York: Rabinowitz.

Leventhal, Dennis A. 1985. "Sino-Judaic Studies: Whence and Whither: An Essay and Bibliography", pp. 36-79 in *Monographs of the Jewish Historical Society of Hong Kong*, vol. 1, Hong Kong: Hong Kong Jewish Chronicle.

Musleah, Ezekiel N. 1975. *On the Banks of the Ganga: The Sojourn of the Jews in Calcutta*. North Quincy, MA: Christopher Publishing House.

Pirke Avoth: The Ethics of the Talmud: Sayings of the Fathers. 1971. Ed. and trans., R. Travers Herford. New York: Schocken.

Roland, Joan G. 1989. *Jews in British India: Identity in a Colonial Era Hanover*, NH: University Press of New England.

Roth, Cecil. 1941. *The Sassoon Dynasty*. London: Robert Hale Ltd.

Sassoon, David Solomon. 1949. *A History of the Jews of Baghdad*. Letchworth: S.D. Sassoon.

Steinsaltz, Adin. 5750/1900. "Mt. Sinai: A Contract with No Escape Clause", *Jerusalem Post International Edition*. Shavuot Supplement, p.1.

Strizower, Schifra. 1971. *The Chidren of Israel: The Bene Israel of Bombay*. New York: Schocken.

Timberg, Thomas. 1978. *The Marwaris*. New Delhi: Vikas.

Timberg, Thomas. 1985. *Jews in India*. New Delhi: Vikas.

Yakkov, Avraham bar. 1965. *Yahudei Bavel Me'Sof Tkufat Ha Geonim ad Yomeinu*. Jerusalem: Ben Zvi Institute. [In Hebrew]

6

Promised Lands and Domestic Arguments:
The Conditions of Jewish Identity in Burma[1]

Ruth Fredman Cernea

It would be easy to miss Musmeah Yeshua, the grand and all-but-silent synagogue in the heart of Rangoon. It stands behind high white walls, on a narrow street filled with vendors of betel leaves, bananas, books, homoeopathic medicines and clothing. From the busy street corners one catches a glimpse of the Sule Pagoda, reputed to be 2,500 years old, an important center of Buddhist worship in this deeply religious land. A few blocks away is the once-elegant Strand Hotel, where dignitaries, royalty and writers stayed when the British ruled the country in the late nineteenth and early twentieth centuries. The hotel is now decaying—seemingly reclaimed, like many buildings, by the incessant press of nature in hot, humid Burma.

But if you turn from the sights of the streets, and raise your eyes, you will see above the white walls an archway decorated with a seven-branched blue candelabra and the name of the synagogue in large blue letters. Surprisingly white and well maintained amid the greying buildings that line the street, the synagogue stands as a testimony to the proud community that constructed it in the late nineteenth century, and to the devotion of the few remaining

[1]This paper is derived from ongoing research beginning in 1987. In addition to the sources documented, I am grateful to the many individuals who have contributed information, time and encouragement for this project, including: Moses Samuels, Jack Samuels, U Aung Kywe, Ruth Sofaer, Judah and Flora Sassoon, Ellis Sofaer, Florence Joseph Shamash, Maurice Shamash, Sally Joseph, Flora Jacob, Joe and Kitty Sassoon, Solly Saul, David Sofaer, Shaul Abraham, Edwin Azariah Samuel, Simon Aaron, Sarah Sassoon Raphaeli, Saul Ezra Saul, Saw Benson/Ben-Zion Koder, and Helen Einy.

Burmese Jews and their friends, who hold it in trust for an uncertain future.

Once the focus of a vibrant Jewish community life in this outpost of the British Empire, Musmeah Yeshua (Heb.: "Brings forth salvation") has witnessed the florescence and decline of Jewish—and British—fortune in Burma, and has endured global war and local rebellions, Japanese occupation and Burmese national ascendancy. Despite the dramatic political flux, Buddhist Burma has been, for the most part, a tolerant home for the Jews for some one hundred and fifty years. Even so, the historical context in which they found themselves has left its mark on Jewish identity in Burma. The Jews of Burma have always been but one minority among the many religions and nationalities that comprise Burma's diverse population. During the years of greatest community strength and satisfaction in Burma, Jewish social definition, as well as internal ideology and dynamics, were responsive to the requirements of maintaining power and position within the changing political and social environment. The glory of those years lingers on in the memories of the remaining Jews of Burma, but in a far different political situation and with far different social definition.

Group self-conceptualization—"ethnic identity"—is a fluid process informed by ideology and history, social context and social encounters. A reflexive dialogue, ethnic identity is never a fixed state but a continuing conversation between peoples who test their world views against the other, concurring or disagreeing, finding areas of commonality or separation, merging or distancing, defining, defending or extending the scope and meaning of personal and group boundaries. The history of the Jews in Burma is a record of many such conversations between the Jews as a community and the diverse populations with which they have interacted. It is also the record of a family argument, of disagreement among the Jews themselves, which would not stay private because it affected the very basic social and ideological identities of Jews within the Burmese context.

East from Calcutta

The first Jew known to be in Burma was Solomon Gabirol, probably a Bene Israel from India, who served as a commissar in the army of King Alaungpaya (1752-60). Calcutta's Baghdadi Jewish opium merchants came, but did not stay, during the early years of the nineteenth century when Rangoon was part of the trade route that linked Singapore, Manila and other ports in southeast Asia.

From the middle of the nineteenth century, Jews and other groups moved into the region to take advantage of the economic opportunities offered by the British umbrella. In the 1840s, two European Jews—a Goldberg from Romania and Shlomo Reinman[2] from Galicia—arrived in Burma to trade in teakwood and remained as merchants and suppliers to the British forces, who had come to Burma in 1824 and were then engaged in the conquest of northern Burma. The majority of the settlers, however, were Baghdadis who came via India or directly from Iraq, and who established themselves in Rangoon, Mandalay, Moulmein, Bassein, Maymyo, Toungoo and other trading points. In 1841, Azariah Samuel, from Bushire on the Persian Gulf, arrived in Akyab—with his *shohet* (ritual slaughterer). Other Sephardi and Iraqi Jews were drawn to the region from Egypt, Syria and elsewhere in the Middle East. Indian Jews—the Cochinis and Bene Israel—came in smaller numbers following Britain's annexation of Burma as a province of India in 1885. Literate in English, these Indian groups remained in Rangoon as clerks and managers for the British and for the Iraqis who, for the most part, could not read or write English well enough for the needs of their trade. Other Bene Israel moved north to Mandalay, where some became railway workers.

By 1853, there were sufficient Jews in Rangoon to organize Burma's first Jewish congregation. In that year, the site of what is now the synagogue property, at No. 85, 26th Street, on the block of land between 25th and 26th and Dalhousie (now called Maha

---

[2]Shlomo Reinman recorded his experiences in Reinman 1884.

Bandoola) Streets, was granted to the Jewish community by the British government, as was land for a cemetery on 91st Street, about two kilometres from the synagogue. Also granted at that time were rights to a building at 66/70 31st Street containing eight apartments (the rights to these lands were extended by the Burmese government after Independence). In 1857, the first synagogue, Musmeah Yeshua, was founded on 26th Street. By 1896, the community had increased sufficiently in size and fortune so that the building could be expanded to its present grandeur.

The synagogue is surrounded by a one-storey building, which houses twenty-seven stalls for small businesses and continues to provide a modest income for the community. In return, the community pays the government quarterly land and municipal taxes.

By 1907, a prayer hall was located in Mandalay, and Mandalay also had its own Jewish cemetery. For a time there were also prayer halls in Bassein and Moulmein. In 1932, Rangoon's short-lived second synagogue, Beth-El, was founded on 31st Street in a building owned by the Solomons. The Jewish community in Burma during this period had the full range of social and charitable organizations, including a Boy Scout troop and a Zionist lodge, and Jews were also members of the local Masonic lodge. The green, red and blue button worn by the Zionist group had a double message: in English it announced "The Rangoon Jewish Association"; in Hebrew, "Rangoon Committee for the Recognition of Israel". Musmeah Yeshua boasted a Talmud-Torah, and its 126 silver-clad Sifrei Torah proclaimed the pride and achievements of the community.

Musmeah Yeshua's Register of Births and Marriages for the period 1880-1900 indicates the founders of the earliest Jewish community in Burma: Ezekiel Hai Solomon Khadoori, Abraham Shalom Jacob Meyer Abraham Cohen, Mordecai Hayeem Isaac Cohen, Joseph Isaac Joseph Said, Meyer Abraham Sofaer, Isaac Solomon Abraham Sofaer, Isaac Ezekiel Isaac Solomon Benjamin, Mordecai Hayeem Isaac Mordecai, Abraham Raphael, Menahem Hai Salah Sassoon, Jacob Meyer Abraham Shemuel,

Saul Isaac Meyer, and Shlomo Rahamim Levi (Moses Samuels, U Aung Kywe 1991:8).

At its height, on the eve of the Second World War, the Jewish community in Burma numbered some 2,500 people, about 2,000 of whom lived in Rangoon. All but a few Jews, about fifteen families, fled to Calcutta in January and February 1942, just prior to the Japanese invasion, huddled on hastily-secured boats with bombs falling overhead, or walking overland across mountains and through swamps on their desperate "passage to India". The few who stayed behind did so out of devotion to their Moslem or Burmese wives, or out of devotion to the community. The care-taker, or *shamash*, of Musmeah Yeshua planned to stay to the last moment, after sending his family ahead. His devotion was to cost him his life.

Solly Saul, who was a child at the time of the outbreak of the war, recalls:

The bombing of Rangoon by the Japanese . . . will not be forgotten. Taking shelter in the stairway of our apartment building, we heard the thud of falling bombs. There were many who were machine-gunned to death as their curiosity found them on the streets. Our dear mother, may her soul rest in peace, was terrified each time an air raid occurred. My father decided to send the family to Myaungmya, an overnight trip by ferry. We stayed with a Chinese family . . . and later with an uncle. Before too long, the British government organized an evacuation—the overland route from northwest Burma into Assam in India. Transit camps were set up for the refugees. The journey, lasting approximately a month, encompassed travel by foot, ferry, sampan, mounted elephants, the last leg of the journey being by train to Calcutta.

My mother, uncle, elderly aunt, sister and twin brothers comprised the first group to leave. My father, my aunts and uncles and their families were scheduled to follow us. Hundreds of refugees, mainly from the European and Anglo-Indian community, were evacuated in this fashion. Details of the trip have almost faded from my memory, but the names of the towns along the route have not—Kalewa, Tamu, Kohim and Imphal. These names are forever embedded in my memory.

Unknown to us, refugees in Mandalay were airlifted to Calcutta after our departure. Imagine our surprise when upon arriving in Calcutta we were met by our own father and others who had remained in Mandalay when we departed!

One child who fell behind on the hasty exit through the mountains was rescued and adopted by a tribal family; reclaimed after the war by a surviving relative, she came with them in great despair, agonizing over losing yet another family. A few families who were living at a distance from Rangoon could not make it to the boats in time and were trapped in Burma during the Japanese occupation. The Japanese spared Isaac Sassoon because of the intervention and pleading of his Karen wife; after the war his wife and children converted to Judaism, the couple was remarried in Musmeah Yeshua, and the family left for Israel, where a son died in the 1956 war. Light-skinned Isaac Samuels, the father of the current synagogue trustees, was suspected of being a pro-British sympathizer.and jailed. Toward the latter days of the war, the synagogue's caretaker, Joseph Shamash, was tortured to death by the Japanese after an informer singled him and another out for making hopeful comments about the advance of the British. Some of the Jews who reached safety in Calcutta returned to Burma during the war as soldiers with the British army in India.

Four to five hundred Jews returned to Burma after the war, but the life they remembered was gone. On January 4, 1948 the British colonial period ended and the independent state of Burma was proclaimed, with Burmese replacing English as the official language. For a short time, it did seem that Jews once more had a future in Burma: the returnees were encouraged by the establishment of diplomatic relations between Burma and Israel and the warm personal relationship between Prime Ministers U Nu and David Ben-Gurion. Even so, in recognition of the diminished community and the problematic political scene, the leaders of the

Burmese Jewish community transferred 42 Torah scrolls and 142 Holy Ark canopies (*parochet*) to Israel in 1955.

The cautious optimism of the returnees was to be short-lived. They had been drawn to Rangoon by memories of a pleasant, privileged life; they found, instead, harsh economic circumstances and repercussions from worldwide political upheavals. For the first time, the Jews of Burma were the target of attack by Burma's Moslems, disturbing the history of amicable relationships among the country's ethnic minorities. In November 1956, Moslems in Rangoon staged street demonstrations against Israel's participation in the Sinai campaign. General Ne Win's 1962 coup and nationalization of businesses further eroded the position of Jews and other minorities in Burma, and accelerated emigration. In 1967, Moslems, angered by Israel's victory in the Six Day War, attacked the synagogue. Although the damage was slight, and the government helped with restoration, fifteen families left the country shortly afterwards, in 1968 and 1969, with the assistance of the community. Florence Joseph Shamash, who had returned to Rangoon from Calcutta, remembers "living in fear" during these years.

Throughout the post-war period, the number of Jews had continued to diminish gradually, through natural attrition and emigration to Israel, India, Australia, the United States and England. In the early 1980s, synagogue trustee Jack Samuels wrote: "Now there are only a few Samuels, Aarons, Moseses, Alberts, Daniels, Davids, Solomons, and Raphaels living in Rangoon, Mandalay, Myitgne, and Bassein totalling about sixty men, women and children in all. All of them are citizens of Burma although they are Jews by race and faith. The Synagogue management committee hands out monthly charity to not less than six heads of family and meets medical and *Osay Hassad* (charitable) expenses for the Jewish community, most of whom are poor and aged and with not enough income to support themselves" (Jack Samuels 1980:2). Upkeep of the synagogue, financial assistance to elderly and impoverished individuals, and taxes continue to strain the resources of the remaining community, especially of the Samuels brothers. In 1980, the Birth and Death Records of the community were transferred for safekeeping to the Central Archives for the History of the Jewish People in Jerusalem by Israeli Ambassador Kalman Anner.

Almost Englishmen

The world of the Jews of Burma at the turn of the century is recalled warmly in his memoirs by Ellis Sofaer, part of the once powerful Sofaer family of Rangoon. Now an elderly gentleman in England, Ellis Sofaer writes:

> I was born in Rangoon at the time when the sun never set on the British Empire. Queen Victoria had died but three years earlier. Britain's greatness shone with brilliant splendour, and the Pax Britannica spread over us like a benign umbrella. It gave us comfort and stability, and it fostered the conviction that God was in his heaven, and all was right with the world.
>
> In the environment into which I was born I was exposed to two cultures. There was the 'public' culture of the British presence, and then again there was the private culture of the Jewish family of which I was a member. This duality did not seem strange to me, quite the contrary. Around me I saw numerous ethnic groups similarly placed, behaving at times in the British tradition, and at others in accordance with their own cultural inheritance. Besides the Burmese, there were Moslems, Hindus, Parsees, Turks, Armenians, Chinese, and others. And there were, of course, Jews (Ellis Sofaer 1987:I, 1).

Mr Sofaer was born in 1904, eighteen years after Burma was incorporated as a province of India. It is more accurate to say that the Jews were in Burma, not of Burma, and that the simple duality of identification described by Ellis Sofaer was a bit more complicated. The community was in fact several subcommunities, differentiated by social status, religious interpretation, and history. The Baghdadis, who formed the upper class, did not intermarry with the darker-skinned, Marathi-speaking Bene Israel, nor did they intermarry with any of the other groups who lived as neighbors on the densely populated streets of central Rangoon.[3] The Baghdadis defined community standards and controlled access to the primary means of validation of Jewish identity, the synagogue. As will be discussed later, their control threatened the very basis of Jewish identity for the Bene Israel in Burma.

The Baghdadis utilized their family connections abroad to become middlemen traders, importing fine foods and other goods desired by the British and others in the international community, or trading in more mundane materials—crockery, textiles, whatever was needed—throughout the Burmese countryside, and servicing the ships that docked in the busy Rangoon harbor. They lived in close and comfortable society on Dalhousie, Merchant, Fraser, Tsekai Maung Taulay, Phayre and the numbered streets in the heart of Rangoon, employing Bene Israel, Cochin Jews, and Hindustanis in their stores, and Hindustanis in their homes. The wealthiest Baghdadis had palatial second homes farther out-of-town, away from the business district. The Sofaer building at the corner of Merchant and Phayre Streets proclaimed the prominence of the Jews of Rangoon; the building was opened officially with a gold key by the Governor-General of Burma. At one time there was a Jewish mayor of Rangoon, a Jewish mayor in Bassein, and a street in Rangoon named after a Jew: Judah Ezekiel Street. The Solomon family donated the bandstand near the Sule Pagoda, and visitors to the Rangoon Zoo passed through gates donated by the Sofaer family.

[3]There were, in fact, a few cases of intermarriage with conversion. Some of these couples presently live in Israel. Some people recall stories of Burmese, Karen or other tribal mistresses—and possibly children of these unions. The community also kept apart from the tribal Jews of the remote northwestern border, who claim ancestry from the "lost tribe" of Menasseh. Currently called the Bene Menase, they are comprised of groups from the Shinlung tribes of Mizoram and Manipur in northeast India, who trace their origins to an area called Shinlung in Sichuan province of China. The Bene Menase believe that the tribe of Menasseh arrived in China after their exile by the Assyrian King, Shalmaneser V. Simon Aaron, who was born in Mandalay in the mid-1930s, recalls his father telling him of his encounter with this "lost tribe" during trading missions to the interior.

Memories of Burma are rich with images of family gatherings, boat parties in the Rangoon harbor, and visits with relatives in the hill regions of Maymyo. They remember Burmese, Chinese and other street celebrations enjoyed from the balconies of Fraser Street, the foods, the homoeopathic medicines, and the sense of well-being life provided in pre-war Burma.

With nostalgia, Solly Saul says:

It was always a desire of mine to return to Burma for a visit. This longing was more than just sentimental—the attachment to the country where one was born is, I am sure, deeply felt by most. Sadly, it is unlikely that I will ever be able to fulfill my dream. . . . And so I must rest content with reliving in my imagination the most happy memories I possess of the city and country of my birth: the peaceful days, the happy and friendly Burmese, the torrential monsoon rains, the rich vegetation, the tropical fruits, the imposing Shwedagon and Sule Pagodas, the City Hall, my school, teachers, and fellow students, my synagogue and my home.

The most prosperous Baghdadis sent their children to the English schools, where they learned Shakespeare, played cricket, and ate kosher lunches carried to the schools by servants. They learned Burmese as one of their other, marginally used, languages. (Since most domestic workers were Hindustani, that language was, in fact, more useful to them than Burmese.) Hebrew was taught at home by private tutors before school each morning or on Sunday. They competed with each other on the teams of the English Diocesan Schools, St. Paul's, and St. John's College. Writing in 1916 in *The Fleur de Lys: The Magazine of the Diocesan Schools*, editor Abraham Sofaer states:

This School is vastly different from the other schools in Burma. The boys are all British, all speak English habitually, and indeed live in an absolutely European manner. Consequently patriotism, which is a feeling and not a science that can be taught in the classroom, is present in the School and needs only to be developed. . . . We have a Company of Cadets . . . whose smartness and efficiency on the parade have earned them a high reputation. . . On Empire Day and on other days of national import, "D" Company turns out to do honour to the Flag and to give three cheers for the King and for the British Empire *(Fleur de Lys* 1916:1-2).

Jewish attendance at English schools required the payment of double fees. This effectively kept out the "less desirables", as defined by the pocketbook. The other Jewish children attended the community's Jewish English School at 22 Sandwith Road, where they also studied subjects useful for the education of a citizen of the Empire and, of course, Hebrew.

As they became English and European by education and culture, the children understood the Baghdadi Arabic of their parents and grandparents less and less. Ellis Sofaer remarks that it became difficult for the younger generation to follow the Passover Seder when the parents, clinging to Baghdadi tradition, recited the Haggadah in Arabic; despite this obstacle the children understood that they were participating in a great and meaningful celebration (Sofaer 1987:III, 5, and personal communication, 1992). As time went by, the prayer books also had to be replaced: the first *siddurim* were in Hebrew and Sharak (Arabic written in Hebrew letters); gradually, as the spoken Arabic became unintelligible to the generations born in Burma, English was introduced into the prayer book.

The families carried British passports and therefore lived as though their future belonged in Europe, even though their past was Middle Eastern and their present Asian. The declaration of the state of Burma in 1948 is recalled by a gentleman now living in Los Angeles in these words: "I became a stranger in the land of my nativity" (personal conversation, Los Angeles, 1989). Yet the land he is talking about—Burma—was never truly his home; his home existed within the international community of Burma and specifically within an England he had never visited. Even so, these

Jewish Englishmen-in-exile were denied entry into the Gymkhana Club where, as Ellis Sofaer describes it, "The worthy gentlemen who carried the burden of the Empire went for relaxation and company" (Sofaer 1987:V, 3). Despite his outstanding record at the English Diocesan School, Abraham Sofaer was passed over for the prize he coveted—the Burma Medal—which guaranteed a place at Oxford for an exceptional gentleman-student from Burma. He suffered a second slight when he was denied a commission in the British army, given almost routinely to his classmates, in the First World War.[4] These were not isolated instances of exclusion; they were reminders of the limitations of British identity for the Jews in Burma. Still, life was good and the slights tolerable, because as Jews the Baghdadis had another identity which offered them stability and security.

Promised Lands and Domestic Arguments

Jewish identity can be conceived of as a refuge, a home, a place of security in an alien world. Distanced spatially from relatives abroad, the Jews in Burma were nevertheless close to them through the orthodoxy of home and synagogue ritual. The rules of Jewish law formed an apparently eternal framework for the society. They kept them true to their past, conforming with Jewish communities elsewhere. The continuity of tradition was ensured by a ritual director from Iraq, who served as rabbi, cantor, ritual circumciser, overseer of ritual slaughter and arbitrator of questions about Jewish law. That the authoritative voice about Jewish law and practice was vested in a representative of Iraqi Jewish tradition was significant for the community. Decisions about religious practice are also implicitly decisions about community definition, since the laws of Judaism also serve as boundaries for the society: the dietary laws of *kashrut* not only express consistency with God's will, but also

---

[4]While he never forgot these affronts to his patriotism, Abraham Sofaer left for England shortly after. He became a well-known actor on the London stage, and later starred in films in Hollywood.

encode the limits of social interaction between the Jew and others. In strict tradition, to break a law is to break a barrier between the community and the outside population, even as a barrier is erected between the Jewish community and God.

Each Sabbath, each Passover, each Yom Kippur, the Baghdadi in Rangoon knew that his cousins in Iraq and elsewhere were lighting candles the same evening, eating *matzah* when he did, and experiencing with him the fast of Yom Kippur. Especially during the early years in Burma, they were united with their past and with their relatives through the special, in-group language of Baghdadi Arabic. And the holy language of Hebrew lifted the Baghdadi even more firmly across time and space, reinforcing his relationship with God as well as with the worldwide holy kinship community. This was, of course, also true of the other Jewish groups, for although the synagogue ritual was Iraqi in practice, the calendar and celebrations are essentially the same for all Jews.[5]

Jewish law and the Hebrew language reinforce the realization of Jewish identity as inherently international and eternal. The transplanted, international language and culture of the British in Burma was easily compatible with this essential Jewish identification. The English, as well as the Jews, were aliens in Burma, and interacted with the local population only when necessary for the transactions of business and daily life. In the international community in which the Jews lived, the Burmese language learned at school was rarely needed: their servants were likely to be Indian, their schooling was in English, they spoke to their parents in Arabic (especially during the early years), and they prayed in Hebrew. Jews and British alike recalled a distant home in myth-like terms: the Jews conceived of the promised land as Jerusalem of Gold; the British envisioned it as the splendid empire

---

[5]Ellis Sofaer writes (1987:3, 1): "It was quite common in the early part of the nineteenth century for Jewish families in the Near East to be sprawled over the different Turkish dependencies like an outstretched net, and yet to remain cohesive. The separate branches chose their centres of activity not from sentiment, but for the trade opportunities they discerned in the territory of their choice; and it is certain that the same attitude motivated the Jews who drifted to India at the time."

ever shining in the golden light of the sun. For the Jews in Burma, Hebrew was the intimate language of home and heritage and English the language of passport and political future, as well as the language of an elusive ideal. Although they turned their face toward England, this was a land they never actually experienced, a promised home presented through the paradox of only partially-opened doors. Yet together, English and Hebrew formed a comforting cocoon around the Baghdadi Jews in their Burmese home.

Affective reinforcements of identity are transmitted at home, a concept even more than an actual place. "Home" suggests comfort, easy acceptance, a place where the person fits naturally. At the quintessential home ceremony, the Passover Seder, the child is initiated into the abstract concepts and fundamental realities of the society through highly sensuous and emotionally charged materials and actions. The *haggadah*, or "narration", of the Seder presents the ideals of exiled community in an eternal and paradoxical relationship with God, but similar messages are carried in the wine the child must drink and the bitter herbs he must swallow. Community is first experienced as extended family and friends. At this level, foods, ritual, and even personal identification are not Baghdadi or even "Jewish": they are home and family.

The synagogue, Musmeah Yeshua, was a home above all homes, and a glorious statement of Jewish identity. Ellis Sofaer notes: "The ability to read Hebrew was necessary if one wished to take part in the synagogue. Each repeated attendance at the synagogue was not so much an act of worship as an assertion of one's Jewish identity" (Sofaer 1987:I, 5). Each person had an assigned place within the building; to this day people raised in Burma remember exactly where their fathers sat, and relive their pride in locating their fathers from the heights of the women's gallery or, for a boy, in sitting with his father in the special family pew. On the eve of Yom Kippur, the synagogue's 126 silver and gold clad Sifrei Torah were displayed around the *bima*, the reading platform for the Torah which stands in the center of the synagogue. Families also donated beautiful embroidered and gilded *parochet* (curtains) for the Holy Ark; each Yom Kippur all of these beautiful cloths covered the tall pillars of the synagogue, thus tangibly and gloriously linking individual families, their heritage and the proud place of the Baghdadi Jews within the British Empire in Burma. The synagogue caretaker knew exactly where each parochet was to be placed each Yom Kippur; the *shamash's* son Maurice, in his home in Los Angeles, can picture his father placing each silk or velvet cloth on the pillar closest to each family's pew, as though it were yesterday.

There were two main sources of support for Musmeah Yeshua: the rents from the synagogue's property, and the selling of synagogue honors. In many traditional synagogues, people bid for the honor of being called to read the Torah, to open the Ark, or to perform other functions relating to the service. The man receiving an honor brings honor to his entire family; in this home of homes, he also declares the relative insignificance of the slights of the outside world.

In this context, to deny synagogue honors has deep implications, for it challenges a family's most basic connection with a worldwide community as well as with a sustaining ideology. In 1913, the Baghdadis established synagogue rules that barred the Bene Israel from approaching the Torah during the seven regular *aliyot* on the grounds that the Bene Israel did not follow a Jewish law (*halitzah*) concerning remarriage of a widow to her dead husband's brother.[6] This ruling, based on Jewish legal principles, therefore challenged the legitimacy of the Bene Israel as Jews, and put in question the kinship between the groups. The Bene Israel refused to modify their practices, claiming that the law in question was contrary to their tradition and did not affect their definition or status as Jews.

Starting in the 1920s, the Bene Israel were also barred from election to the synagogue Board of Trustees. In 1934, after their names were also struck from the list of voters, the Bene Israel sued

---

[6]This argument about the levirate marriage was also part of the conflict between Bene Israel and Baghdadi Jews within other parts of India.

the synagogue—and won. In his judgment on April 9, 1935, Justice Leach said:

> 'The plaintiffs claim that the Bene Israel are members of the Jewish faith and community . . . The defendants deny the validity of this claim and say that the Bene Israel are not of the Jewish faith or community . . . because they do not observe the Mosaic law with regard to divorce, *yibbum* and *halitzah*. . . . It is admitted by the defendants that the modern Jew refuses to marry his brother's widow and openly disobeys Mosaic law in this respect . . . and the *halitzah* ceremony has been modified . . . and consequently it cannot be said that failure on the part of the Bene Israel to observe this law would make them unorthodox. There is no doubt that the Bene Israel in Burma have for many years been looked down upon by other Jews in the Province. . .' (Cowen 1971:177-79).

It was a judgment of Civil Regular Suit No. 85 of the High Court of Rangoon that "there is no evidence worthy of the name in contradiction" that the Bene Israel are not Jews and that the "Defendants are not entitled to exclude from the lists a Jew merely because he is a Bene Israel" (Cowen 1971:179). The legal framework of the British Empire thus intruded into the private space of the synagogue and the two main correlates of Jewish identity in Burma came together, upsetting for the first time the control of the Baghdadis over the conditions of Jewish identity.

The argument between the Baghdadis and the Bene Israel was much more than a disagreement about a rather infrequently employed traditional prescription. It was also a question of status, and a means through which the more aristocratic, fair-skinned Baghdadis might further separate themselves from the darker-skinned Bene Israel and thus ensure their own position within the ranks, according to the codes, of the colonial empire.

The highest status in Burma, of course, belonged to the British, who defined its terms. The elite Baghdadis approximated the British as best they could, retaining an elite Jewish identity while acquiring the British language, schooling, and passports. The British acknowledged the Baghdadis' sophistication, and used their abilities as capitalists, traders, purveyors of luxury and necessary items. Yet, ultimately, the British locked the doors of the country club. The Baghdadis' position was pleasant—even luxurious and exciting—but also ambiguous and insecure, dependent upon British grace.

In this position, the Baghdadis apparently felt the need to "purge" from close identification any group that might lower their status vis-a-vis the British, and thus threaten their acceptance in the new society. But much as they tried, the Jews remained useful but marginal to the British, not quite "white" enough in this color-conscious society. And as time went on, the wealthier Baghdadi children raised in Burma became less and less a part of traditional Baghdadi Jewish experience. Placing greater distance between themselves and the Bene Israel—and the "lower classes" of Baghdadi families also—seemed an unspoken strategy for closing the gap between themselves and the British. Similar distancing can be described between Jewish populations in many parts of the world.

The Bene Israel were able to withstand the assault to their identity as Jews within Burma because they were, in fact, an extension of the strong Bene Israel community of India proper. Less organized Jews were not as successful. It would seem that it was humiliating to be a poor relation of the Baghdadis. During our interview, a now-elderly woman who lived this situation before moving with her parents to Indonesia steadfastly refused to discuss her childhood in Rangoon; she preferred to recall her subsequent internment in a Japanese prison camp. Another man, a Cochini who was orphaned as a child in Rangoon, disassociated himself from the Jewish community. He married a Karen woman, converted to Christianity, and became a leader in the Karen secessionist movement. His daughter Louisa was the first Miss Burma. Yet deep inside, he tugged at his Jewish roots, affectionately recalling his Jewish parents and his grandfather, a community leader in Cochin—and then, to the amazement of his new wife and Burmese daughter, retrieving from the bottom of a drawer in his home in Wheaton, Maryland, the papers attesting to his parents' marriage and his birth, as recorded in the archives of Musmeah Yeshua.

Aftermath

The cataclysmic political events following the Second World War have left few Burmese Jews in their wake. Today, Musmeah Yeshua exists as a testimony to filial piety and a public assertion of the more private identity of the few remaining, mostly elderly, Jews. The Samuels family—brothers Jack and Moses, and Moses's family—still reside in the 31st Street property, and serve as trustees of the synagogue. Musmeah Yeshua's two remaining Sifrei Torah were donated by their father, who died in 1978. Moses Samuels has three teenage children—the youngest Jews in Burma today. The synagogue and community are maintained through the contributions of the Samuels family, by the rents collected from the synagogue's stalls, and through contributions from abroad. The community has been without a rabbi since 1969, but has been helped by the Israeli Embassy in conducting religious services at Rosh Hashanah and Yom Kippur, and during the infrequent times when there are enough visitors to form a *minyan*, or quorum. The community also maintains the cemetery in Rangoon, periodically cleaning the underbrush from its 700 rounded, huddled tombstones, but no one is left in Burma who can carve Hebrew on the newer stones. Assisting in caring for the synagogue and cemetery is a longtime Burmese friend of the Samuels family, U Aung Kywe, whose watercolor posters of Jewish holidays and announcements of prayer times enliven the entrance and walls of the quiet building.

There are few other recurrent reinforcements of Jewish identity. In fact, intermarriage with Moslems and Burmese, and the distance from sources of Jewish learning and community, have blurred the consciousness and understanding of Jewish identity in Burma today. Worldwide Jewish organizations, Israel, and occasional visitors are the lifeline for the Burmese Jews, sending them donations, Hanukkah candles, *matzot*, and other reminders of their heritage. Yet a visitor who walks past the street vendors of 31st Street will come upon a house set apart by a *mezuzah* on the doorpost, with walls lined with posters from Israel, and meet a young boy, not Jewish at all by the definition of the Baghdadis who built the synagogue, who will greet them with a shy "Shalom". In winter 1993, Sammy Samuels became a bar *mitzvah* amid the tall pillars and embedded memories of Musmeah Yeshua, joining his ancestors and linking the Jewish future in Yangon, Myanmar.

Sources cited

Archives. Musmeah Yeshua Synagogue, Rangoon, Burma.

Birth and Death Records of Musmeah Yeshua Synagogue, kept at Central Archives of the History of the Jewish People, Jerusalem.

Cernea, Ruth Fredman. 1988. "End of the Road: The Last Burmese Jews," *B'nai B'rith International Jewish Monthly*. (June-July): 26-30.

Cowen, Ida G. 1971. *Jews in Remote Corners of the World*. Englewood Cliffs, NJ: Prentice Hall.

The Fleur de Lys: The Magazine of the English Diocesan Schools. Edited by Abraham Sofaer. Rangoon, Hanthawaddy Printing Works, and The Rangoon Times Press. (April 1916-March 1919).

Franks, Suzanne- 1987. "The Lost Tribe of Manipur," *The Jerusalem Quarterly*. London 3: 32-35.

Kamm, Henry. 1980. "Burma's Last Few Jews Living on Proud Memories," *New York Times* (August 10): 6.

Katz, Nathan, and Ellen S. Goldberg. 1988. "The Last Jews in India and Burma," *Jerusalem Letter* 101 (April 15): 1-8.

——————. 1989. "The Mysterious Chin-kuki Tribal Jews of the Indo-Burmese Border Region," *Journal of the American Association of Rabbis*. 5/1: 11-19.

Parasuram, T.V. 1982. *India's Jewish Heritage*. New Delhi: Sagar.

Rabin, Keith W. 1982. "In Burma, Getting a Minyan Together

Even on Yom Kippur, Is Not Easy," *New York Jewish Week.* (July 11): 8.

Reinman, Shlomo. 1884. *Masa'ot Sholmo b'Erets Hodu, Burman v' Sinim [The Travels of Solomon in the Lands of India, Burma and China].* Vienna: Schur.

Samuels, Jacob. 1980. "Appeal to Jewish Brethren Far and Near." Rangoon: Musmeah Yeshua Synagogue.

Samuels, Moses, and U Aung Kywe. 1991. *Musmeah Yeshua Synagogue and Jewish Community in Burma.* Rangoon: Musmeah Yeshua Synagogue.

Shanson, Lindsay. 1988. "Lost and Found: The Jews of Burma," *Israel Scene.* (July): 8.

Sofaer, Ellis. 1987. "Gaya: His Childhood." London, Unpublished memoir.

Twentieth Century Impressions of Burma. 1910. London, India Office Library and Records.

Yegar, Moshe. 1984. "A Rapid and Recent Rise and Fall," *Sephardi World.* (July-August): 8.

Part IV

Indian Jewry Since Independence

7

Marginality and Community Identity Disintegration among the Jews of India*

Margaret Abraham

This paper is a study of the Jews of India—namely the Cochin Jews of Kerala, the Bene Israel of Maharashtra and the Baghdadi Jews of Calcutta.[1] Based on interviews conducted in 1987-88 with one hundred and seventeen informants from these three communities (31 Cochin Jews, 46 Bene Israel, and 40 Baghdadi Jews), this paper explains the nature of marginality and community identity disintegration of the Indian Jewish communities in contemporary India. For such an analysis it is important at the very outset that we clarify how the concept of marginality is defined within the context of this paper.

The sociological literature on marginality has been restricted primarily to the explanation of the personality type and its application to sub-cultural or ethnic groups within the socio-psychological framework, or to explain urban and economic characteristics in Latin American countries.[2] Definitions of marginality have ranged from characterizations of the marginal man, one who is a 'cultural hybrid' in terms of his 'two different worlds', (Park, 1928), the 'crucible of cultural fusion', (Stonequist, 1961), the State 'where one has ties to two partially incompatible societies and one does not belong wholly to either' (Antonovsky, 1956), or the social situation where members combine the components of being economically

---

[1]For historical and ritual details of these communities see Strizower, 1971; Roland, 1989; Timberg, 1986; Johnson, 1985; Musleah, 1975; Fischel, 1962, 1961-62

[2]Park, 1928; Stonequist, 1935; Dickie-Clark, 1966; Slotkin, 1943; Antonovsky, 1956; Mangin, 1967; Portes, 1972; Perlman, 1976.

deprived, non-participants in political activity and lacking integration in the mainstream of society.

Drawing from the literature on marginality and elaborating on
it, I have attempted to construct a body of generalizations which
forms the framework for the analysis of marginality among the
Indian Jewish communities. Thus marginality can be defined as the
social situation which arises:

i)   when there is contact between two disharmonious cultures
in the same setting;

ii) when there is perceived as well as real domination of one
culture (the non-marginal group) over the other (the marginal
group):

iii) when there are partially permeable boundaries which
allow the subordinate or marginal group partially to internalize
the norms and values of the dominant culture and at the same
time are excluded from total membership of that culture, both
actually and symbolically; and

iv) most significantly, when this social situation is manifested
by the dominant group forming the core and the subordinate
groups being allocated a peripheral positioning in the spatial,
social, economic and political structure of the setting.

In this analysis, then, the concept of marginality is based on the
peripheral positioning of the subordinate or marginal group due
to its function of having the elements and orientation of two
disharmonic cultures, while simultaneously being denied total
membership from both these cultures. It is important to note that
here marginality means partially belonging to both cultures rather
than belonging totally to one. The concept of marginality in this
analysis is primarily from the perception of the marginalized group
and of their situation in the social setting. It is crucial to understand
that the concept of marginality is not absolute but a matter of
degree. Groups can be marginalized with respect to some spheres
of life but be well integrated in other spheres. Thus the Indian

Jewish communities can be discussed in terms of their differing degrees of marginalization and community disintegration in contemporary India.

The nature of marginalization and community identity disintegration can be best understood through an analysis of: (1) the setting in pre- and post-independent India and emigration factors; (2) the spatial, social, economic and political positioning of Indian Jewry in contemporary India; and (3) marriage and religious practices among the remaining Jews in India today.

The Setting

The early part of the twentieth century witnessed an increased momentum in India's nationalist movement. It also witnessed the establishment of the Zionist movement in India. These two movements played a pivotal role in determining the Indian Jews' perception of their ethnic identity and how they perceived themselves as being defined by "others". It resulted in a heightened awareness among the Indian Jews of their Jewish identity, as well as an awareness among them that the dominant majority was mainly protecting its own interests. In pre-independent India, the Jewish minority, especially the Bene Israel and the Baghdadi Jews, had occupied a privileged position under the patronage of the British. In keeping with their policy of divide and rule, the British had favored the minorities who were numerically too small to pose a political threat to British supremacy. As Gussin states in his study of the Bene Israel:

"They were favored by the politics of insignificant numbers. Precisely because the community was so small and, therefore, presented no threat to the British overlords, it was disproportionately rewarded."(Gussin, 1972:72-74.)

While there had always been a certain degree of boundary maintenance between the Indian Jews and the other communities, it was a harmonic coexistence. It was harmonic in that the boundaries were a function of the caste structure. The principles governing the caste structure had been internalized by all communities, including the Indian Jews, thereby allowing the smooth flow of social interaction. The nature of this interaction was changed by the British. Through their quota system for the minorities and their patronage on the basis of minority status, they had stimulated among the Indian Jews a sense of distinctiveness vis-a-vis the Hindu and the Muslim population. Under the British, the Indian Jews were encouraged to manifest and articulate an ethnic identity which could not be defined within the caste framework. Religious differences became the focal point in defining ethnic identity and the marker for cognition and behavior in social interaction.

The economic opportunities provided by the British and their access to education under the missionaries had placed the Indian Jews in an advantageous position. The attainment of this position was also a visible marker of the ethnically defined differences between the Indian Jews and the rest of the population. In return for the patronage they received from the British, the Indian Jews remained loyal to the British. Even the Cochin Jews were indirectly aligned to the British, since the Maharaja of Cochin had signed a treaty with the British in 1809 whereby Cochin would enjoy peace and protection under British suzerainty. Thus the departure of the British was perceived by the majority of Indian Jews as the end of a golden era—an era in which patronage had inproved their socio-economic status.

The ethnicization of their Jewish identity and its reinforcement through the Zionist movement in India deflected the Indian Jews from active participation in the Indian nationalist movement. Having been the recipients of a privileged status under the British, the Indian Jews were reluctant to oppose them by joining the nationalist movement. The intense effort by Zionist leaders had influenced the Indian Jews to express their Jewish identity through the Zionist movement. The formation of various Zionist organizations in India from 1905 onward provided the necessary means to shift to a Jewish nationalism rather than an Indian one. The means and goals for the majority population and the Jewish minority were not defined in any common terms. The identification with Zionism and simultaneous lack of active participation in India's struggle for freedom, at a time when it was the central issue for the dominant population, were to have indirect political and economic ramifications in Independent India. The privileged minority position of Indian Jewry under the British, their primary identification with the Zionist movement, and the articulation of a predominantly Hindu identity by the dominant Indian population in the struggle for an Independent India, thus provided the initial setting for the emigration which followed the establishment of Independent India and the creation of the State of Israel (Abraham, 1991).

Having briefly discussed the setting, we may now proceed to an analysis of the spatial, social, economic and political positioning of Indian Jewry in contemporary India.

Spatial Structure

Geographically the dominant Hindu communities and the Indian Jewish communities are not separated on ethnic lines. Among the Cochin Jews, the majority are members of the Paradesi section and as such continue to reside on Synagogue lane in Mattanchery. The community has lived there for many centuries under the patronage of the Maharaja of Cochin. Since this area has a heterogenous population and the members of the community are not restricted in terms of geographic mobility, they do not perceive themselves to be spatially marginalized. However, today, except for the houses in which the present members of the community live, all the other houses which had Jewish occupants have been bought as shops by Hindus and Muslims due to the increasing commercial value of this area. Although it is fast becoming a commercial area, it is the desire of the members of the community to continue to reside in this area, close to their famous synagogue.

Both the Baghdadi and Bene Israel communities live in large metropolitan areas which are characterized by a mixed population where economic factors are the basic criteria for determining group locations. Hence neither the Bene Israel nor the Baghdadi Jews can be defined as spatially marginalized on ethnic criteria. Due to the exorbitant cost of housing, the majority of the Bene Israel, like lower middle class members of other communities, have moved to the suburbs and outskirt towns of Bombay. The wealthy among the Bene Israel continue to live in the city; those not so well-off live in poorer neighborhoods. In the case of the Baghdadi Jews, too, economic criteria determine the nature of housing, though in many cases they continue to reside in homes that have been owned by their family for many years. Thus we may say that the Indian Jewish communities are not spatially marginalized on ethnic lines.

Social Structure

In the social structure of India today, the Cochin and Bene Israel communities do not perceive themselves to be marginalized. There is considerable social interaction between them and the non-Jewish population. This is indicated by the nature of social interaction and each community's perception of their own status. Among the Cochin and Bene Israel informants, more than 80 per cent have frequent or some interaction with non-Jewish communities. Similarly their closest friends tend to be both Jewish and non-Jewish Indians. In terms of their community's social status vis-a-vis the social structure, the majority of the Cochin informants placed their community's social status as "somewhat high". In the case of the Bene Israel, the perception of the community's status was perceived by the majority as "somewhat low". Although both the Cochin and Bene Israel have social interaction with the dominant community, their differences in perception of status stemmed from their previous historical circumstances and were also related to their respective economic situation. The following quotes, by a Cochin and a Bene Israel Jew respectively, demonstrate this:

> "In Kerala, our community has quite a high status because from early times, we were protected by the Maharaja and

given many privileges. Some of our people had important economic positions. Today, though most of our people have left and we are so few who remain, we are still treated with respect. This is because of our long tradition of a good position in Cochin."

"I think that we Bene Israel don't have a very high social status as a community. Some individuals may have but not the whole community. In early times our people did not have a high caste job... then with the British there was some improvement, but the Baghdadi Jews said all kinds of things about our community which were not good for us. Also, we don't have lots of wealthy people in our community. So neither way we could really have a high position. It is not easy to change a community's social position. It cannot happen in a few years."

Among the Baghdadi Jewish community, there appears to be the strongest sense of marginalization. This is indicated by the nature of their social interaction with non-Jewish communities and their perception of their community's status in India today. Among the Baghdadis interviewed 80 per cent "rarely" or "never" socially interact with the non-Jewish Indian community, nor do they interact socially with members of other Jewish communities. Over 88 per cent of them perceive their community's present status as "somewhat low" or "extremely low". This is considered by the informants a consequence of their loss of prestige, with the departure of the British and the wealthy Baghdadi members of the community, coupled with the rise of a big business community among Hindus.

Thus we see that socially the Cochin and Bene Israel do not perceive themselves to be marginalized, while the Baghdadi community do. This is primarily due to the nature of their articulation of their identity in the context of India today. In the case of the Cochin and Bene Israel, their Indianness has helped in their partial social integration. On the other hand the Baghdadi community manifests an identity which is in disharmony with the dominant culture and as such is quite marginalized.

Economic Structure

There has been substantial industrialization and technological development in India since India's independence in 1947. Yet India's economic structure today is still characterized by tough competition for scarce economic resources, inflation, over-population, poverty, insufficient employment opportunities and housing problems in the major cities. Attempts by the Hindu majority to establish its hegemony, despite a constitution which promises equal rights for all citizens, has resulted in the economic marginalization of the minority groups. For minuscule minorities like the Indian Jewish communities, among whom a large percentage had previously prospered under the British patronage, open competition with the numerically dominant majority has resulted in their being squeezed out of the economic system. Hence, the majority of them have perceived emigration as the best alternative, thereby drastically reducing the number of members in each of the Jewish communities of India today.

In the overall economic structure of India today, the Indian Jewish communities as an ethnic minority are almost totally marginal. They do not play any significant role in India's economy and have been relegated to a peripheral position. Among the Cochin and Baghdadi Jewish communities, a large percentage of the members are retired and hence without any occupation.

Among the Cochin Jews, more than a third of the sample have no formal occupation. This has further lowered the standard of living in this community. The household incomes indicate that with the exception of a small percentage who have a high household income, the majority are in the lower middle range in the economic structure. However one has to remember that today the Cochin community primarily comprises the Paradesi Jews who have always been economically better off than the large Malabari section of the Cochin Jewish community who emigrated *en masse* to Israel. Hence in today's India, the Cochin Jewish community cannot be defined as totally economically marginalized. This is also reflected in the members' perception of the community's economic status. The informants appear to be divided in their perception of their community's status in the larger economic structure. Approximately half view the community's economic status as "somewhat high" and the other half view it as "somewhat low". The former view can be attributed to the few wealthy members in the community, whose economic prestige is perceived by informants as enhancing the community's economic status. In the words of one informant:

"Previously we had a high economic status but I don't think that is the case today. Our community is too small to have any economic significance. Although there are the ... who are well known and rich, that does not mean that the whole community has a high economic status today. Many of us are retired and the few youngsters are leaving [emigrating] and one of the reasons is for better economic opportunities. Today there are a number of other very rich people in Kerala and our economic importance has almost disappeared. Those who tell you otherwise are living in the memory of the past."

We may then state that although the economic situation of the Cochin Jewish community has declined, the members who comprise the community today, unlike the majority of those who emigrated, are not totally economically marginalized. Rather it is their small numbers coupled with an ageing population that have affected their economic situation.

Among the Bene Israel, the majority are concentrated in occupations in the lower and middle economic ranges. The high cost of living has necessitated many families to have more than one earning member in the household to provide an adequate income. As an ethnic community, the Bene Israel have a relatively low economic position. As in all communities, there are those members of the community who earn high incomes or hold prestigious jobs and at the individual level have a high socio-economic status, but these members are few in number and do not necessarily identify or interact with the larger Bene Israel community. Ninety-one per cent of the Bene Israel informants perceived their community's economic status as "somewhat low" or "extremely low" vis-a-vis the dominant communities, thus indicating their economic marginalization.

In the words of a Bene Israel informant:

"Our economic position as a community is not high because here there is too much competition and our community is too small to be able to compete with many of the other groups. Also, today influence and money are both very important in getting a high status. Our community don't have either. Each community only tries to help their own people."

For the Bene Israel then, a perception of economic marginalization vis-a-vis the dominant community in the economic structure still persists. However this may also be due to the high cost of living in Bombay and the lack of correspondingly high incomes.

Today the economic situation of the Baghdadi Jewish community in Calcutta has deteriorated to a large extent. Among the Baghdadi informants, 73 per cent had no occupation. Sixty-three per cent had no earning member in the household and were supported by the Baghdadi Jewish Trust founded earlier by the wealthier members of the community. Today funds from this trust are distributed among the needy members of the community, though a considerable portion of it is tied up in litigation with the Indian government. Approximately 60 per cent have a total annual income of less than $999 which has resulted in a very low standard of living for the majority. There are still a few wealthy members in the Baghdadi Jewish community and some of these members play an important role in helping out the poorer and ailing members. Today, as an ethnic community, 37 per cent and 63 per cent respectively of the informants perceive the economic status of the community as "somewhat low" and "extremely low". There is a strong feeling of economic marginalization. Most of the members feel that their community was much better off under the

British. There is a common sentiment among the community that the Indian government has not looked after its interests and that it is the dominant Hindu population that controls most of the economic power. As stated by a Baghdadi informant:

"Most of us Baghdadi Jews today are in a bad economic situation. There are many old, ailing and poor among us. Only some of our own people like the ... help the poor and sick. The Indian Government does not make it easy for this community. It has withheld our own community trusts. At present the case has been taken to court. Some of the members will most probably die before it is all settled. Just because we are a small minority they can do this to us. We are too old to leave this country now. Besides who will want to accept old and sick people? There is nothing left for us here."

We see that among the Baghdadi community in India today, there is a strong sense of economic marginality. In general, we see that in today's overall economic structure, the Indian Jewish communities as an ethnic minority are economically marginalized, though the extent varies with each community.

Political Structure

The political marginalization of the Indian Jewish communities since India's independence was one of the causal factors for their emigration. The departure of the British, and the subsequent shift in the Indian political structure from a system based on the patronage of the minorities to one based on adult franchise, signified the end of preferential treatment for minorities. Communities which were numerically strong and could draw upon the loyalties of their members could attain political power. On the other hand, minuscule minorities like the Indian Jews were marginalized due to their insufficient numbers. With most of the Indian Jews having opted out of the Indian society through emigration, the political status of these communities in India has

deteriorated considerably. Today, it is apparent that the Indian
Jewish communities are unable as an ethnic minority to act as a
viable political entity. The communities are characterized by a
high degree of powerlessness and political apathy. This is indicative in the informants' lack of membership in organizations, either
Jewish or political, and in their perception of their community's
status vis-a-vis the dominant community in the political structure.

Among the Cochini and Baghdadi informants, 94 per cent and
90 per cent respectively are not members of any Jewish
organization but among the Bene Israel there is a lower percentage
of informants who are not members of such organizations. None of
the Cochini and Baghdadi informants and 87 per cent of the Bene
Israel participated in any political organizations or activity. With
reference to their community's status in the political structure of
India today, a high percentage in all three communities expressed
it as "somewhat low" or "extremely low".

For the Cochini and Baghdadi informants, lack of membership
and perception of a low status vis-a-vis the dominant community in
the political structure is based on their view that their respective
communities are too small, with a predominantly aged population,
who are no longer in a position politically to revitalize these
communities. This view is expressed in the following statements
by a Cochini and a Baghdadi informant respectively:

"Look, most of the Cochin Jews have left. The few young ones
remaining will also leave soon. With only a few members and
most of us being old, there is no meaning in getting involved
in any organization. Politically we can assert absolutely no
influence even if we do get involved, so what is the use? Politics
in India today is for those who can influence lot of people and
often votes are bought off by parties. There is nothing that a
handful of us can do and neither do we have the energy or the
means. Today the Cochin Jews have no position in politics."

"Today our community is a dying community. We are old and
are unable to do anything. Political parties know they can get
nothing from us, we are too small a community to make any

difference to them. It is sad that today we are no longer an important community in India... there was a time under the British when our people were close to those in power, but that has all changed. Now we have no connections with those in power, they are more interested in those communities whose vote will make a difference in winning or losing. There is no doubt that the political position of our community is very very low. In fact it can be said that today the Baghdadi Jewish community is politically dead!"

Among the 46 per cent of the Bene Israel informants who are members of Jewish organizations, participation is confined to socio-religious activities revolving around the synagogue. This too is infrequent and tends to be for the organization of the cultural activities of the community for specific Jewish occasions. Eighty-seven per cent of those interviewed were not members of any political organization, thus indicating a high level of political apathy. Here lack of participation in political organizations or political activity was based on the perception that the political parties were not interested in such a small minority. Informants felt that their involvement in political activities would not change anything since the dominant Hindu majority asserts all the control and power. As put by a Bene Israel informant:

"Our community has no power and the political parties don't trouble us. We are no threat to them. Our people don't want to get involved in politics. They know so few of us will not change anything and instead create problems for us only. Today our community has given up any hope of having any political power."

Thus today these communities have become non-viable political entities in articulating their interests. This perception of their non-viability as even a pressure group was indicated by informants when mentioning the Government of India's attitude to Israel. India's large Muslim minority, coupled with India's economic interests in the Arab world, have negated any chance for this microscopic Jewish minority to bring pressure on the Indian government to change its foreign policy with respect to Israel. As stated by a Cochin infomant:

> "Being Jews, we would like India to improve its relations with Israel. With such a large Muslim population and the government's trade relations with the Arabs, they are being too cautious. Sometimes we wish as a community we could influence the government but we know that that is impossible, there are just too few of us to make them change their policies."

Thus we see that all these Jewish communities in India experience a sense of powerlessness in the present Indian context and this powerlessness is strongly related to their numeric insignificance. There is a perception that the smallness of their numbers has increased their political marginalization. This has resulted in many demonstrating political apathy and thus opting out of the political structure.[3]

Finally, we may proceed to the last section of our paper. Having referred to their varying degrees of marginality, we can now turn to community disintegration. This is best explained through a discussion of the problem in the sphere of marriage and religious practices among the remaining Indian Jewry. It is important to examine these two dimensions as they were the primary channels through which the Jewish identity of these communities was maintained as the basis for community integration.

---

[3]As this research was conducted well before the establishment of full diplomatic relations between India and Israel in February 1992, it remains to be seen how this significant development will affect the Indian Jews' sense of political marginalization. See "A time of joy for Indian Jews", *Indian Express Sunday Magazine* (February 16, 1992).

COMMUNITY DISINTEGRATION

Marriage

For the Indian Jewish communities, prior to the emigration of the majority of their members, marriage was a means of boundary maintenance. The normative order among Jews prescribes marriage and building of a family governed by the Judaic principles and as such places a high value on marrying Jews as opposed to Gentiles. The adherence to the normative structure by marrying members of one's own community thus reinforced community solidarity and was a boundary marker. Today among the Baghdadi Jews it is no longer a means of articulating a Jewish identity since there are no young, unmarried members in the community. In the case of the Cochin Jews, the desire of the few young members left in the community to marry Jews, preferably members of their community, has partially influenced their decision to emigrate, and this indirectly demonstrates their desire to adhere to the Jewish normative structure as well as to reinforce their Jewish identity through marriage. In both these communities in India there has not been a marriage in the past ten years. This itself speaks for the disintegration of the community structure.

Among the Bene Israel marriage is indicative of both their Jewishness and Indianness. The Bene Israel in India prescribe marriage within their own community. In those cases where the woman is not Jewish and is selected as a partner in marriage by a Jewish male, she is first converted to Judaism. However many of their marriage customs are similar to those practised by the Hindus and Muslims of their region, and as such are defined by them in terms of their Jewishness and Indianness. Among the younger generation today, there is increasing secularization of marriage. While conversion to Judaism of the spouse does take place, the religious strength of those converted is sometimes perceived as questionable.

Religion

During their centuries of stay in India, especially in the eighteenth, nineteenth and first half of the twentieth century, it was the Judaic content of their culture which made the Indian Jewish communities distinct from the mainstream Indian society. Although incorporating some customs from the core culture of Indian society, it was the manifestation of their Jewish identity through synagogue attendance, observance of Sabbath, Jewish holidays and dietary regulations, which differentiated the Indian Jewish communities from all others. The synagogues were the pivotal axis around which the organization of the community revolved. High holidays were observed by the members of the communities and were socio-religious occasions which expressed the social solidarity of the communities.

Today, it is still through the observance of rites and rituals that community solidarity is maintained. Moral commitment is expressed through the adherence to the normative order of Judaism, though there has been some degree of adaptation to external and internal forces of social, economic and political change. Among my Cochini informants, 77 per cent strictly observed Sabbath while 23 per cent did so partially. As for synagogue attendance, 65 per cent went every week. Today, due to the sharp drop in their numbers, the Cochin Jewish community has a problem obtaining a *minyan*. However, for high holidays and other festivals there is full attendance. It is during these holidays that the community visibly articulates its solidarity.

During Passover, strict boundaries are maintained between Jews and others (Katz and Goldberg, 1989). It is a key festival in sustaining the family and community solidarity. The moral commitment of the members of the community is expressed in their adherence to Passover despite the difficulties faced by them in obtaining the necessary ritual ingredients. Rosh Hashana, Yom Kippur, Succoth, and Simchat Torah are all observed by the Cochin Jewish community. Today there have been some modifications necessitated by their small numbers and the unavailability of certain materials essential for Jewish ceremonies. However, despite the changes brought about by the constraints that have arisen over time, the Cochin Jewish community still observes these holidays. The consequence of adherence to these rites is a reinforcement of community solidarity and the identity of the community. Unlike the Cochin Jews, only 26 per cent of the Bene Israel informants strictly observe Sabbath, 63 per cent partially observe it, and 11 per cent do not observe it at all. This changing pattern among the members of the community is a result of the constraints imposed by the urban environment in which they live. For example, in India Saturday is a part of a six-day work week and therefore it becomes difficult to observe it as a day of rest. Synagogue attendance among the Bene Israel community tends not to be too frequent. Among my Bene Israel informants, the majority went either several times a year or only for the high holidays. The holy days for the Jews are observed by the Bene Israel, and it is during this period that the community come together and articulate their community solidarity through collective social action.

Through the collective celebration of the religious ceremonies, members of the community become conscious of the social and moral force of the collectivity. There thus occurs the recreation and reaffirmation of social solidarity, making these occasions important markers of a Jewish community identity. Today the Baghdadi Jewish community is not as observant as the Cochin and Bene Israel. Among the Baghdadi informants, 32 per cent strictly observe Sabbath, 50 per cent partially observe it and 18 per cent do not observe it. Those who partially observe are not particular about switching on lights or cooking. As put by an informant,

> "Earlier our community used to be very, very orthodox. Now this is not the case. For example, I cook and switch on lights. Most of the members of the community don't observe Sabbath strictly. It is hard these days. Many of us live alone, have to do own work. There does not seem to be much choice."

The holidays are still observed by a majority of the members.

The preparations are not elaborate but it is the only time when most of the members get together and when there is some degree of community solidarity.

An important part of the religious norms of Judaism are the dietary regulations. It has been said, "The dietary laws have proved an important factor in the survival of the Jewish race; and are, in more than one respect, an irreplaceable agency for maintaining Jewish identity in the present" (Hertz, 1954:960).

For centuries, an important dimension in the articulation of the "Jewishness" of the Indian Jewish communities has been in the observance of the dietary regulations prescribed by Judaic law. Today it continues to be one of the most important ways through which two of the three Indian Jewish communities articulate their Jewish identities.

For the Cochin Jewish community today, the observance of the Judaic dietary regulations plays a very important role in articulating their Jewish identity. Among the Cochin informants, 70 per cent stated that they strictly observed dietary prohibitions while 30 per cent stated that they partially observed them. Here partial observance was indicated by not observing all the dietary laws or deviating from them on occasion. All who were interviewed strictly observed the separation of milk and meat and 87 per cent strictly observed the restrictions on seafood. Religious orthodoxy and the strong desire to maintain what they perceive as an important aspect of their Jewishness is demonstrated by the Cochin Jewish community who, because they have no *shochet* (the ritual slaughterer who is qualified to butcher cattle), abstain from eating mutton or beef. The separation of milk and meat and the restrictions on eating only those fish that have fins and scales are also strictly observed by the members of this community.

The use of alcohol in traditional Judaism is an important prescriptive norm: so it is incorporated in the activities of the social group and used as an expression of family and community solidarity (Snyder, 1973:6-19). In the making of wine for ritual purposes, the Cochin Jews are extremely particular about separating the sacred from the profane. According to the Judaic law, wine used by Jews should be made only by Jews. This stipulation stemmed from the fact that in other religions, wine was used to consecrate idols and as such was forbidden to Jews. It is assumed that if Gentiles make or touch the wine, they may possibly dedicate some of this wine to their Gods (Asheri, 1983:138). Among the Cochin Jews, wine for ritual purposes is made by the members of the community. Since the wine is for ritual purposes it is treated as if it were sacred. Hence if this wine were to be touched by a Gentile or even the table or shelf on which the wine is kept is touched by Gentile, the wine is perceived by the Cochin Jewish community as "profane". Thus, since the separation of the sacred and the profane is perceived by the members of the community as the avoidance of contact between the wine and the Gentile, it becomes a boundary maintenance marker. Yet it is these very important rituals that are becoming increasingly difficult for the Jewish community to maintain.

The observance of the dietary regulations for Passover represent important rites for all Jews. Through their strict adherence to the dietary norms of Passover, the Cochin Jewish community expresses and reinforces the important sentiments of community solidarity and boundary maintenance. Central to the observance of Passover is that anything that has leaven, chamets, or hamas as the Indian Jews pronounce it, or which may come into contact with hamas, is forbidden. The Cochin Jews, primarily the women, are extremely careful in cleaning all of the items of traditional food which will be used during Passover. Preparations to observe the dietary regulation and the other requirements for Passover, start about three months prior to the event.

Among the Cochin Jewish community the dietary regulations concerning the avoidance of hamas are strictly adhered to despite the difficulties and expenses involved in it. Their dietary regulations during this period heighten their articulation of a Jewish identity. The extreme concern with "purity" during Passover tends, in certain ways, to resemble the principle of purity, pollution as observed by the Hindus (Katz and Goldberg, 1989:301-325). However, the members perceive it as their strict adherence to the normative order of Judaism. It is apparent from the above that the Cochin Jews do articulate their Jewishness through their observance of the dietary norms and maintain social boundaries with the other communities through tangible expressions of avoidance of the profane. Yet today this community struggles to maintain these manifestations of their ethnic identity and have had to make some compromises in these processes of purification.

For the Bene Israel, too, dietary regulations play a central role in boundary maintenance and social solidarity. Among the Bene Israel informants, 77 per cent strictly observed dietary prohibitions while 23 per cent observed them partially. As in the case of Cochin Jews, there were no informants who did not observe any of the dietary prohibitions. Since this community is still large enough to support the services of *shochets*, the Bene Israel continue to eat mutton. However, it has retained the Hindu custom which had been adopted by the earlier settlers of abstaining from beef. Although it was prohibited earlier, prior to the discovery of their Jewish identity, despite their knowledge of the Judaic dietary laws they voluntarily avoid eating beef today. However, besides the adoption of this Hindu practice in their dietary regulations, the Bene Israel strictly adhere to the Jewish dietary laws and as such reinforce their Jewishness in a predominantly Hindu social environment.

The separation of meat and milk in cooking and eating is strictly followed by the members of the Bene Israel community. Among my Bene Israel informants, 90 per cent claimed they strictly observed the separation of meat from milk and 10 per cent said they observed it partially. As regards prohibition of seafood, 87 per cent said they strictly observed it and 13 per cent said they observed it partially. However, where they differed from the Cochin Jewish community was that many of the members did not maintain two separate sets of crockery for eating. This was explained as resulting from financial and space constraints. In the words of an informant,

"Among the poor, they cannot afford two different (sets). It is also difficult to keep separate plates where there is no space, children come and mix it up. Besides meat and milk things are never cooked at the same time and each time anything is used it is washed carefully so there is no mixing. We are careful about seeing to this."

With reference to seafood, the Bene Israel once again, like the Cochin Jews, articulate their Jewishness by eating only kosher fish. They kept this practice even during the period when they were isolated from mainstream Jewry.[4] In fact it is perceived by them as an important indicator of their Jewishness. As an informant put it :

"Even when our forefathers forgot parts of our religion, they still kept to the practice of separating fish that have fins and scales and those that did not. It is an important part of our history (as it contributed to their re-entry into Judaism). Today we still follow this law carefuly. We do it becuase it is said in our holy book that we must do it."

In accordance with the Judaic law, for ritual purposes the Bene Israel use wine solely made by Jews. The making of wine is done both at home and communally, the latter done frequently with the mutual cooperation of the members of the synagogue. Here too, great care is taken by the members to preserve the ritual purity of the wine. In a communal setting in which women make the wine, there is a strong proscription against participation of women who are ritually impure. No members outside the Jewish community are involved in the wine making. This assures the purity of the wine. It also becomes a boundary maintenance marker. Passover dietary regulations are also carefully observed by the Bene Israel.

The Baghdadi Jews in Calcutta, although an orthodox community that strictly adhered to the Judaic dietary regulations for many centuries, are no longer as strict today in their observance of the

---

[4] This "fish story" can be read in Israel, 1984:12, 56 or in Roland, 1989:12.

Judaic dietary laws. Among the 40 Baghdadi informants, 35 per cent claimed they strictly observed dietary prohibitions, 35 per cent said they partially observed them and 30 per cent said they no longer observe them. Similarly, regarding maintenance of a kosher kitchen, 37 per cent strictly observed it, 30 per cent did so partially and 33 per cent did not observe it at all. Today there are no *shochets* left in this community so kosher mutton or beef is not available. There is, however, one man who is qualified to kill chicken.

Thus, among the few families who are still orthodox, only chicken is eaten. Unlike the Cochin Jews, many of the members do not observe the fish restriction and in some cases they also eat non-kosher meat. However it must be remembered that today a large percentage of the Baghdadi community cannot afford to eat meat and fish on a regular basis due to the high cost of these products. Those who partially observe some of the dietary prohibitions tend to do it by the separation of milk and meat or by not eating leaven at Passover. Only those who strictly observe dietary prohibition, maintain a kosher kitchen.

In this community, wine making is not a communal activity, nor is it done in the homes of most of the members. Those few who can afford wine get it from abroad. Passover among the Baghdadi Jewish community is not as important as in the other two communities, though it is observed by the members. Little is done by the majority, except abstaining from eating leavened food and having a Seder. The lack of observance of the dietary laws is attributed by this community to the constraints of old age, ill health and economic necessity. Today there is a weakening in the bonds between the members and the community. Most of the members who remain in India are single. Hence the family as the mediating structure between the individual and the community no longer exists. This has indirectly contributed to a weakening in community bonds.

Conclusion

We can conclude that in the culture of the Jewish communities in India today, there are varying degrees of observance of the Judaic content. Maintaining religious practices has become increasingly difficult despite attempts to retain them. In general, there is a decline in the articulation of a Jewish community identity. This decline is most apparent among the Baghdadi community as a result of the weakening of community bonds. In all three communities Passover is still a key festival in sustaining the community identity, yet it is only a shadow of what it used to be prior to the large scale emigration from India.

We may then conclude that all the Indian Jewish communities express a dual identity within the present Indian context, although the nature of this duality varies to a certain extent, thus resulting in different degrees of marginalization across these communities. An ethnic minority, marginality is most visible in the economic and political structure. Their dwindling numbers and the preponderance among the Cochin Jews and the Baghdadi Jews of the elderly has resulted in a social disintegration of the Jewish communities in India. It is apparent that within a short period of time there will be a total disintegration of these two communities. Although the Bene Israel in Maharashtra, especially in Thana, have tried to maintain their Jewish identity, forces of urbanization and secularization may result either in their gradual assimilation into the dominant culture, may resurge as a viable and active Jewish community or like the rest of their members, they may emigrate to Israel. Only time will tell.

Sources cited

Abraham, Margaret. 1991. "The Normative and the Factual: An Analysis of Emigration Factors among the Jews of India", *The Jewish Journal of Sociology*, Vol. XXXIII, 1: 5-19.

Antonovsky, Aaron. 1956. "Toward the Refinement of the 'Marginal Man' Concept", *Social Forces* 35, 1:57-62.

Asheri, Michael. 1980. *Living Jewish*. New York: Everest House.

Dickie-Clark, H.F. 1966. *The Marginal Situation: A Sociological Study of a Colored Group*. London: Routledge & Kegan Paul.

Ezra, Esmond David. 1986. *Turning Back the Pages: A Chronicle of Calcutta Jewry.* 2 vols. London: Brookside Press.

Fischel, Walter. 1961-62. 'Early Zionism in India'. Reprint from *Herzl Year Book* 4:309-328.

—————. 1962. "Cochin in Jewish History: Prolegomena to a History of the Jews of India", *American Academy for Jewish Research Proceedings* XXX:37-59.

Gussin, Carl Mark. 1972. "The Bene Israel: Politics, Religion and Systematic Change". Unpublished Ph.D. dissertation, Syracuse University.

Hertz, Joseph. 1954. *Daily Prayer Book.* New York: Bloch Publishing.

Johnson, Barbara Cottle. 1985. "'Our Community' in Two Worlds: The Cochin Paradesi Jews in India and Israel". Unpublished Ph.D. dissertation, University of Massachusetts.

Katz, Nathan and Ellen S. Goldberg. 1989. "Asceticism and Caste in the Passover Observances of the Cochin Jews", *Journal of the American Academy of Religion* 58,1:301-330.

Mangin, William. 1967. "Latin American Squatter Settlements: A Problem and Solution", *Latin American Research Review.* II:65-98.

Musleah, Ezekiel N. 1975. *On the Banks of the Ganga: The Sojourn of the Jews in Calcutta.* North Quincy, MA: Christopher Publishing House.

Park, Robert. E. 1928. "Human Migration and the Marginal Man", *American Journal of Sociology.* 33, 6:881-93.

Perlman, Janice E. 1976. *The Myth of Marginality: Urban Poverty and Politics in Rio de Janeiro.* Berkeley and Los Angeles: University of California Press.

Portes, Alejandro. 1972. *Rationality in the Slum: An Essay on the Interpretative Sociology.* Los Angeles and Berkeley: University of California Press.

Roland, Joan G. 1989. *Jews in British India: Identity in a Colonial Era.* Hanover and London: University Press of New England.

Slotkin, J.S. 1943. "The Status of the Marginal Man", *Sociology and Social Research.* 28, 1:47-54.

Snyder, Charles. 1973. "Orthodox Jewish Drinking Patterns", in

The Substance of Sociology, Ephraim H. Mizruchi (ed.), New York: Appleton, Century, Crofts.

Stonequist, Everett. 1935. "The Problem of the Marginal Man", *Sociology and Social Research*. 41, 1:1-6.

Strizower, Schifra. 1971. *The Children of Israel: The Bene Israel of Bombay*. Oxford: Basil Blackwell.

Timberg, Thomas, ed. 1986. *Jews in India*. Sahibabad: Vikas Publishing House.

* I am grateful to the publishers of *Ethnic Groups,* Gordon and Breach Science publishers, for allowing me to take sections from my previously published article entitled "Ethnic Identity and Marginality Among Indian Jews in Contemporary India." The research of this study was funded by the American Institute of Indian Studies, University of Chicago; The Memorial Foundation for Jewish Culture; The Roscoe Martin Fund; and the Syracuse University Senate Grant, to which organizations I am grateful. I also gratefully acknowledge the valuable comments and suggestions given by Ephraim H. Mizruchi, Gary Spencer, Susan Wadley, Barry Glassner, T. N. Madan, Annie Mathew and Pradeep Singh. A very big debt is acknowledged to the members of the Indian Jewish communities, especially the Koders, Erza Moses and family Nissim Talkar and the Nahoums.

Notes on Contributors

MARGARET ABRAHAM is Assistant Professor of Sociology at Hofstra University, Hempstead, New York. Her dissertation was "Ethnic Identity and Marginality among the Jews of India" (Syracuse University, 1989). She has presented her work on the Indian Jews at various conferences. Her publications include: "The Normative and the Factual: An Analysis of Emigration Factors of the Jews of India" in Jewish Journal of Sociology (1991) and "Ethnic Identity and Marginality Among Indian Jews in Contemporary India" in Ethnic Groups (1991). Her current research in on marital violence in the South Asian community in the United States.

RUTH FREDMAN CERNEA is an anthropologist and currently Director of Research and Publications for Hillel in Washington, D.C. Her publications include the book, *The Passover Seder: Ajikoman in Exile* (1981-1983); a study "Cosmopolitans at Home: An Anthropological View of the Sephardic Jews of Washington, D.C." (1982); "Flaming Prayers: Hillula in a New Home" in J. Kugelmass, ed., *Between Two Worlds: Ethnographic Essays on American Jewry* (1988), and articles on Sephardic and other Jewish communities. Since 1987 she has been conducting research on the Jewish community of Burma, in Burma and abroad. She received her Ph.D. at Temple University, has taught there, and has served as consultant to the Smithsonian Institution.

ELLEN S. GOLDBERG is a journalist, currently Editor of *The Jewish Press of Tampa*. She co-authored *The Last Jews of Cochin: Jewish Identity in Hindu India* (1993) and *Ethnic Conflict in Buddhist Societies: Sri Lanka, Thailand and Burma* (1988) with her husband, Nathan Katz, as well as a number of articles on Indian Jewry and one on Singhalese Buddhist art. Previously she was editor of *The Voice of the Physically Challenged*, associate editor of *Tampa Bay Metro Magazine*, a South-Asia-based contributor to *The Christian Science Monitor* and a reporter for the North Adams (MA) *Transcript*. She is an alumna of Skidmore College.

SHIRLEY BERRY ISENBERG, an alumna of Radcliffe College; Research Scholar at Madras University Anthropology Dept. 1956-61. During her fifteen years in India she studied especially the boatpeople of Kashmir, change in occupation and status of women in South India, and the Jewish communities of India. In New Delhi she served as Resident Consultant to the Educational Resources Center of the New York State Department of Education, and she was Associate Administrator of the India Program of the Maxwell Graduate School of Syracuse University. Her published writings include: "A Window of India, A Teacher's Manual" (1967); "Indian Nationalism and India's Jews" (1988); and "India's Bene Israel, A Comprehensive Inquiry and Sourcebook" (1988). She now lives in Kiryat Tivon, Israel.

BARBARA C. JOHNSON is Assistant Professor of Anthropology at Ithaca College in Ithaca, NY. She collaborated with Ruby Daniel to write *Long Ago in Malabar: Memories of a Cochin Jewish Woman* (Forthcoming), and several articles. Dr. Johnson is the author of "Cochin Jews and K'aifeng Jews: Some Thoughts on Caste and Patrilineage, Community and Conversion" (1995) and "The Emperor's Welcome: Reconsiderations of an Origin Theme in Cochin Jewish Folklore" (in Timberg, 1986). Her earlier work on the Cochin Jews included a Ph.D. dissertation, "Our Community' in Two Worlds: The Cochin Paradesi Jews in India and Israel" (University of Massachusetts, 1985), and an M.A. thesis, "Shingli or Jewish Cranganore in the Traditions of the Cochin Jews of India" (Smith College, 1975).

NATHAN KATZ, the editor of this volume, is Professor of Religious Studies at Florida International University in Miami. Among the books he has written and/or edited are: *The Last Jews of Cochin: Jewish Identity in Hindu India* (1993); Tampa Bay's Asian Origin

Religious Communities (1991); Buddhist Images of Human Perfection (2nd ed., 1989); Ethnic Conflict in Buddhist Societies: Sri Lanka, Thailand and Burma (1988); Buddhist and Western Psychology (1983); and Buddhist and Western Philosophy (1981). He received his Ph.D. at Temple University and served on the faculties of Williams College and Naropa Institute.